URBAN
SOUL
WARRIOR

URBAN SOUL WARRIOR

self-mastery in the midst of the metropolis

LALANIA SIMONE

SOFT SKULL
Brooklyn

Library of Congress Cataloging-in-Publication Data

Simone, Lalania.
Urban soul warrior : self-mastery in the midst of the metropolis / Lalania Simone.
p. cm.
1. Awareness. 2. Cities and towns-Religious aspects. 3. Self-help techniques. I. Title.

BF311.S5678 2008
158.1-dc22

2008017337

ISBN (10) 1-59376-212-7
ISBN (13) 978-1-59376-212-4

Interior book design by Elyse Strongin, Neuwirth & Associates, Inc.

Printed in the United States of America

Soft Skull Press
An Imprint of Counterpoint LLC
2117 Fourth Street
Suite D
Berkeley, CA 94710

www.softskull.com
www.counterpointpress.com

Distributed by Publishers Group West

10 9 8 7 6 5 4 3 2 1

This book is dedicated to my soul sis, Jlove,
for seeing this book within me.

contents

introduction

URBAN SOUL WARRIOR is a manual for the soulful city dweller traversing through the wonders and dangers of the concrete jungle. City life can be a rough and raw experience. We are faced with so many daily challenges and stresses, like struggling to keep up with the bills while gas and food prices keep rising, and keeping ourselves healthy despite the pollution in our environment. Those who are financially comfortable often find themselves absorbed into the endless rat race of maintaining their lifestyle. Our day-to-day experience is so chock-full of schedules, commitments, and the money chase, it's no wonder we are left feeling exhausted and unfulfilled. We have gotten so caught up in the mundane repetition of the seemingly endless struggle, exerting so much energy and effort to get somewhere or be something, that it's easy to see how we have become distracted and forgotten who we really are.

And yet, even through this mental fog of chaos and confusion, there is a feeling—something deep within you is asking for your attention. Your true essence, your divine and infinitely powerful self, is calling to you and asking you to acknowledge the magic and the miracle that you are, the miracle that all of life is.

Urban Soul Warriors are those who are determined to unearth their divinity in the midst of the mad metropolis. Soul Warriors are ready to acknowledge their sacred self, and are discovering the ability to manifest a powerful existence. Urban Soul Warriors have chosen to embark upon a path of self-discovery, even amongst (or maybe because of) the madness of the city experience. They are discovering that life is throbbing everywhere, even within the steel overhead and the concrete underfoot.

Urban Soul Warrior is an interactive book about living an extraordinary and powerful life, about becoming aware of the miraculous state of existence we are living. Humans are in the midst of a spiritual transformation, a great awakening. Smack dab in the middle of the urban experience, we "city folk" are becoming self-aware. Our collective consciousness is growing and unfolding as we begin to understand the vastness of our power, potential, and our connection to ALL. We are the powerful architects of our lives, often moving on auto, not always knowing or believing in our full potential. When we choose to tune into ourselves, to give ourselves the love and attention we deserve, we will see a wonderful reflection, a harmony in our outer lives and relationships. Everyone around you benefits when you love up on yourself. We can't help but become more amazing and abundant as we connect with our limitless essence, and create our lives from this divine and infinite space. Life becomes wonderful when we learn to seamlessly incorporate the ritual of conscious living into our busy lives.

divine, *noun:* proceeding from God or a god, *adj:* heavenly; celestial, surpassing excellence, the spiritual aspect of humans

As our awareness expands we learn to search for seeds of birth and growth in every situation. We have tremendous power and unlimited opportunity to do and be whatever we can imagine. We have access to the ultimate tool of creation and manifestation, the mind. Many have yet to realize that incredible power exists in thought, and that we use this power every day to design our sometimes wonderful and juicy, sometimes boring or unhappy lives. When we become attentive to our thoughts and patterns we are able to break free of unhealthy habits and forge new pathways in our internal and external worlds.

TOPICS

▶ Spirituality: connect with your infinite self and the Source

▶ Self/Body: nurture and heal yourself and your temple

▶ Mental: use the mind to consciously create your experience

▶ Relationships & Sexuality: engage in transformative relationships

▶ Wealth Consciousness: nurture abundance consciousness

how to use this book

This is a workbook, a tool, to manifesting your amazing life. It breaks down some of the science, techniques, and tools used in the conscious creation of your daily life. You will find suggestions on how to integrate this knowledge to transform the daily grind into an incredible journey. Trust your inner self to guide you. The aim of this process is to peel the layers of past influences off of your present moment, helping you to understand and access your own power, and thus manifest your extraordinary life.

Warriors, you are encouraged to write in this book, anywhere and everywhere. Write freely and with abandon. Be honest and truthful with every question and exercise. The word *exercise* means to put into effect. With these exercises we put our power and intention into effect. Thoughts lead to feelings, feelings lead to actions (in this case exercises), actions lead to results. If we don't follow through with our inspired thoughts and actually activate them, we won't see results as quickly as we could. Doing this warrior work puts the information into action immediately. This book is intended to help you incorporate powerful rituals into your day, bringing more of what you'd like to experience into your life. Creating your magnificent life is a joyful experience. You can take pleasure in the assignments that have been provided, knowing that you are planting magical seeds in the garden of your existence.

In the center of the handbook blank pages have been provided so that you may journal, write lists, expand on workbook exercises, record your dreams, doodle, draw, write coincidences and feelings, or whatever you feel like using them for.

Are you ready? Let's do this . . .

THE SOUL
WARRIORS ARE
GATHERING

Urban Soul Warrior, *noun:* one who is determined to unearth his or her divinity in the midst of the mad metropolis; one on the path of self-mastery }

spir·it·u·al, *adj.*: of or pertaining to the soul, to sacred things or matters; religious; sacred; relating to God or Source }

got soul?

SOUL WARRIOR sisters and brothers, what does it mean to have soul? In urban terms it means to have flavor (pronounced flay-va), a certain funkiness whose origins are perceived to come from a deeper kind of cool. We have all heard of soul music, or soul-food. These terms represent a feeling of depth in relation to what they are describing.

We all have soul. Some of us are more aware of it than others. A soul is the self-aware essence unique to each living being. It is an individualized expression of the Universal Presence, of life itself, constantly unfolding to reveal more of the infinite. Or another way to put it: a soul is life experiencing itself through one of billions of expressions.

More and more people are connecting with themselves and the universe at the level of the soul. Unsatisfied with the results they are getting by dealing primarily with the material world, they are journeying within. How do we get in? What is in there, anyway? It has been said that we are not in the world, the world is in us. Discovering the meaning of this is a spiritual journey. Spirituality is the personal relationship with the universal spirit that resides within all life. Through that relationship we can experience an ever-expanding capacity for love and an infinite unfolding of consciousness.

For some the path of the Soul Warrior begins with a desire for an intimate relationship with the *essence* or *spirit of life,* which some may call God. Here, most often, we will refer to the all-encompassing energy of life as the Source, or Universal Presence, to free it from its religious implications. Other seekers long for a deeper meaningful connection with themselves, the Earth, and others, aside from any belief in God or a Universal Presence. There are infinite paths to awareness and awakening, regardless of belief systems.

The ego is the part of the self that seems to oppose unification. It is the mental body that ingests information and files everything away, in effect creating separation.

Being on a spiritual path also refers to the process of releasing the power the ego (a.k.a. the lower self) has had over one's life, resulting in a deeper connection with life as a whole. The ego is driven by the intellect and instincts of mere survival. It is controlled by fear. The ego is a part of the soul that identifies completely with the body and the material world. In order for it to maintain its identity it judges everything and everyone as outside of itself and not itself, thereby creating the illusion of separation.

Soul Warriors are hearing the whispers of their authentic selves and are ready to turn up the volume of their potential power. By consciously instituting simple practices and rituals into our daily lives we can experience a powerful alignment in the many aspects of our existence. As our awareness expands we begin to see any so-called issue or problem as an opportunity to release more limitations, to broaden our understanding of our infinite nature. When we begin to comprehend how what we experience in our external reality is dictated by the confines of the mind, we can then effect our personal experience.

Your spirit is calling you . . .

ritualistic

Integrating uplifting rituals into your day can have a powerful impact on your life experience. The idea is to incorporate practices that you resonate with, as these will be the most effective.

If you are a particularly busy person, it is even more important to find a way to fit activities and spiritual exercises into your life. Busy people often leave themselves out of the equation. Try starting your day with the quick *rise and shine* meditation from Chapter 6. Throughout your day ground yourself or set intentions or say affirmations (Chapter 2). The important thing is to create ritualistic habits. We've all heard the saying that it takes thirty days to make or break a habit. By habituating these powerful rituals, we make incredible strides. Transformation takes focus and dedication, and all dedication takes is making a decision and following through.

Some ideas and exercises in this book may work for you; some, of course, will not. When there is something in particular that you really want to explore or work on, then make a decision to be active about that subject for a period of time. Maybe you can decide to do a certain exercise, meditation, or worksheet every day for seven or fourteen days, make it your ritual. If you really want to see transformation happen in certain areas of your life, attend to the subject with a longer period, say thirty or ninety days. Whatever you decide, make sure that it is enjoyable. Empowering yourself should never feel like a chore. If it begins to feel like nothing more than another task to complete, make some changes to the ritual itself to add interest, or find something else that is fun and effective.

CHECK THE TECHNIQUES

OFTEN WE GET so caught up with the way things are that it's hard to see past our problems and struggles. We can't imagine things being any other way. When we get into the habit of creating time and space for ourselves we can begin to affect our daily experience in a profound way. As you move deeper into this warrior workbook you will need to acquaint yourself with three basic manifestation techniques: meditation, intention, and visualization. These tools offer many gifts, one of them being a moment of presence between you and your life. In city life, quality "me time" can be rare, not because it is unavailable, but because we may be unfamiliar with how to use it effectively. After a busy day, or if we are weighed down with worry and stress, it seems easier to turn on the TV (brain drain) than to give ourselves the attention we need. These techniques can be used for conscious creation or to uncover hidden aspects of ourselves, or simply for relaxation. They are wonderful ways to connect with the creative power of the universe. Once you familiarize yourself with these methods you can easily use them wherever you are.

The following ideas and exercises are suggestions only. Follow where your heart leads you. Use your own methods whenever you like. Or create new ones! The journey begins.

meditate, don't hesitate

Meditation. There's that word again. "What exactly is the point of meditation?" many of you might be asking, "and what's it got to do with me?" There are endless ways to describe what meditating is and what it does. It can be used for cultivating mental discipline, as a means of gaining insight into yourself and the universe, of communing with God or your higher/inner self, or simply for relaxation.

Who couldn't use more relaxation, a clearer head, less stress, and a healthy mind and body? Many of us have dreams and aspirations that seem unreachable through the madness of mere survival mode. Conscious creation takes focus and attention, both of which you have access to through the medium of meditation.

There are different types of meditation, such as: seated meditation, walking meditation, guided meditation, listening meditation, and so on. A deep, seated meditation is best done in a quiet place where you won't be interrupted, but you may find moments for quick and powerful meditations almost anywhere; at work or on the train or bus, depending on your needs.

● ●

Meditation is the key to your connection to the spirit self. It offers an opportunity to align with your essence, to witness your divinity. It is the basis for spiritual transformation. In these moments you are able to reach into your deepest self, and dig out any old ideas or beliefs that have hindered your progress thus far, removing and releasing unwanted emotions and memories. It is a wonderful expression of self-love, as it is a moment you take for yourself. It can be a tool for healing the self or others. Meditation is a vehicle for prayer. It is a way to tune in to yourself and your needs and to the Earth. It is also a great way to connect with other souls, on this plane or others.

People are sometimes turned off by the idea of meditating. They think it takes certain skill, or maybe that it's boring. Most often this is because of so-called failed attempts at meditating. Do not be deterred by anyone's rules about the correct way to meditate; trying to live up to someone else's idea or standards can be frustrating. This is your process, your practice. Do what comes naturally to you. If in your attempt to meditate and connect with yourself you are only able to do so for a few breaths, you have succeeded. Next time it will be a few more breaths, and next time a few more. Meditation is a practice, not a means to an end. Meditation takes place when you turn your attention inward. When you can observe and reflect upon your mind, your breath, your life, your love, silence, beauty, pain, whatever. Meditation occurs when it is your intention to meditate, whether you are able to be silent with a clear head, or you are focused on something in particular. Meditate as you sit or lie quietly contemplating your wondrous self.

Meditation can also be practiced in movement; this is a different experience than sitting meditation. Sitting still for periods of time takes discipline, where moving meditations can be incorporated into almost any time and place. Practice walking meditations—be in the present moment as you meander through the park; experience a connection with the Earth and trees. Or close your eyes for the length of your bus ride, imagining the entire bus full of light. Meditate as you do a series of physical movements such as yoga, becoming aware of each breath, moving with precision. Or move your body wildly, grooving and dancing your meditation; lose yourself in the music, letting your body and internal rhythm guide you.

If when you meditate it is your intention to find silence of the mind, don't be deterred or frustrated by the thoughts that pass through the mind. Allow and observe these thoughts, and do not judge them. When you realize your mind has wandered, gently bring your attention back to the breath. You are not your thoughts; you are the Divine Being that has realized that your mind has wandered into thought! Be joyful! It may take practice, but it is worth the effort. Meditation is your most powerful tool; from it you have access to your infinite self.

Finding a quiet place to meditate can be a challenge, especially if you live in a congested urban area or near a subway line, or if you have noisy neighbors or housemates. Instead of trying to shut out all the sound surrounding you, incorporate it. Listen to all the sounds, feel them, and allow them. Notice how the mind is constantly identifying them with words and names. Try to listen to the sounds without labeling what they are. Be the sounds. If the noise is really disturbing, put on some soft music without words and allow yourself to flow with the music. You may even find that you filter it out and don't even notice it after a time.

● ●

This warrior workbook has many suggestions for meditation. Use them as they are or use them as templates or ideas for creating your own ways to meditate. Creating a daily practice will profoundly impact your life. Try starting with ten minutes a day and naturally increase the length of your meditation as it becomes more natural to do so. If you can't seem to get to it every day, do it as often as you feel is right for you. There are tons of books on meditation techniques and traditions for you to explore if you decide you really dig it. And if you decide meditation isn't for you, that too is fine; there are many other excellent tools and exercises you can still benefit from in this book.

essential meditation

The essential meditation is often the easiest way to become attentive to the natural intelligence, peacefulness, and wisdom that lie beyond our thought process, and so is a great way to begin any meditation exercise. In this meditation you focus your mental attention solely on the breath. The Sanskrit word *prana* describes the breath of life, which is not just the air, but is the life-sustaining energy of living beings. In this meditation we can imagine drawing prana into ourselves, bringing light and love into our being.

{ **Prana** is a Sanskrit word that refers to the vital life force of living beings. It sustains both the body and the mind. The breath is a vehicle for prana. By the practice of pranayama one may learn to control one's prana by controlling one's breath.

SIT IN A comfortable position. Close your eyes and take a few long, slow breaths. Imagine that each breath is perfect life-giving energy. Observe the breath as it enters your nose, and feel your chest expand. Exhale. Notice the moment before the breath enters and after the breath leaves the body. If you like, contemplate the wonder of the breath, realizing that the body's systems move in perfect synchronicity, that all cells may share in the air or life energy brought into the body by the breath. Allow your breathing to establish a natural rhythm; do not try to control it, just observe. Imagine that the mind is an ocean, thoughts are like the crashing waves and turbulence on the top of the water, but deep down the water is still and serene. Dive deep into the breath, and when you keep your awareness on the breath you will dive into your essence.

When you are ready, give thanks for the breath of life, and open your eyes.

If while you are meditating you feel yourself being resistant to it, welcome the resistance; ask yourself, can I be the space for this resistance right now? Resistance is a feeling like every other feeling. Resisting resistance does not make it go away. Allow and acknowledge your resistance without judging yourself. One method that can help create a feeling of acceptance is to tighten the muscles in your body, one at a time or all at once, and then release and repeat until you feel the resistance melting away.

foundation meditation

Many of the meditations in this book begin with grounding and centering. Grounding gives a strong foundation on which to practice a variety of other types of meditations. Centering is creating harmony within yourself, your circumstances, and your environment. The foundation meditation is a great way to start any meditation as it allows you to clear unwanted, stressful energies from your energy body before going on to do other warrior work. Consider the foundation of a house; if it is cracked the house will be unstable. Creating a foundation for meditation allows for more focus, which in turn lends even more power to your intentions. When we are grounded and centered our daily lives are smooth and flowing. Things, ideas, and opportunities just come to you.

The following is a guided meditation that opens an awareness of our relationship with the Earth. It is important to honor our Earth. Every material thing we have and use to experience this life is made up of Earth stuff. As urbanites we often forget about nature. In cities, our Earth is often covered with concrete, tar, and steel. There are more lampposts than trees and the closest body of water is the public pool. But it is important to realize even these things; cement, plastic, and whatnot, are created from ingredients found here on Earth. We are constantly surrounded by Earth, whether we realize it or not.

As you begin to start meditating, you will notice how much the mind has a tendency to wander. Do not be discouraged. When you notice thoughts arising during your meditation you can simply notice them, or say "peace" or "thank you for sharing" and gently bring your attention back to the breath. The important thing is not to judge yourself or get frustrated with your mind—it is through acceptance of our thoughts, rather than resistance, that they actually start to quiet down.

FIND A QUIET place to be. Sit on a chair with your feet on the floor and your hands on your knees. If you like and it is comfortable, you may sit with your legs crossed, hands on the knees. Be aware of your posture. Comfort is important and you may lean on the back of a chair or pillow. Be sure that you are not hunching your shoulders. You want to expand the chest, not contract it.

Close your eyes and begin to breathe deeply. Become aware of your breath and feel it flow in and out of your body. When you are ready, visualize either a cord of light or a root coming out of the base of your spine. Imagine it going straight into Earth. If you live on the eleventh floor of a high-rise, send that root straight down through all the apartments under you until you can imagine it has reached down into the Earth. Imagine that it grows and continues moving until it reaches the center of Earth. Feel your connection with the Great Earth. Experience a sense of safety and comfort.

You may use this cord to release stressful energies or thoughts. Ask the Earth to recycle these energies. You may ask Earth to ground you and guide you in your daily life, or ask the Earth or the Sun to fill your energy body or aura with light and love (we will be doing more of this in a future chapter). Visualize green Earth energy entering your feet and filling your energy body with light and love.

When you are ready, give thanks again and open your eyes.

When doing this meditation and using it to release any unwanted energies, it is a good idea to remember to visualize energy from the Earth or the Sun coming through the feet or head to fill you with light and love. When you empty yourself of stressful feelings you may fill back up with the same type of energy you've just released if you don't make a conscious effort to bring in the type of energy you want to have.

*   *   *

grounding without meditation

A great thing about this grounding exercise is that you can have access to this energy cord or root at any time; it is always available to you. Whenever you need some centering, whether out on a morning jog, at a stressful business meeting, or on a hot date, just remember your cord and reaffirm your connection with Earth. Change the cord regularly by imagining you are releasing it.

You can also create your own way to ground or center yourself if that feels better for you. Follow your intuition.

> "Meditation is the tongue of the soul and the language of our spirit."
> —JEREMY TAYLOR

say what?

Intention and affirmation involve using words or thoughts in a particular pattern or order to manifest a desired result. These word patterns are spoken, written, and/or thought about repetitiously until one has created a new mental pattern that attracts a certain type of vibration, such as a material item or circumstance, or creates a desired change in habits, emotions, or character. They can also be used to affect and heal others, humanity at large and the Earth.

Words are very potent, as they are thought energy and sound vibration together. It is very important to consider carefully what words to use when creating an intention or affirmation. Releasing these divine word combinations into the silence of meditation is extremely powerful.

} **in-ten-tion,** *noun:* an act or instance of determining mentally upon some action or result, to have a plan or a purpose.

```
"It is my intention to attract prosper-
ous opportunities."
"I intend to exercise and eat healthy
meals today."
```

You can begin your day by setting intentions about how you would like to see the day unfold, or set intentions about the things you would like to see or experience in your life.

} **af-fir-ma-tion,** *noun:* the assertion that something exists or is true. To state something as true.

```
"I always attract abundance."
"I am healthy and whole."
```

A mantra is similar to an affirmation. Traditionally used in Hinduism and Buddhism, it is a word or formula chanted or sung as a prayer. An affirmation repeated over and over is also considered a mantra.

Affirmations and mantras are phrases you can say and think to yourself all day to change and create new mental patterns.

For intentions and affirmations to work for you they must be worded in the positive. Do not use negatives in the formulation, even if you are trying to release negatives.

FOR EXAMPLE:

```
It is my intention to pay my debts.
```
(debt is a negative)
```
I intend to live a life filled with
abundance.
```
(abundance is a positive)
```
I am financially free.
```
(free is a positive)

There is an affirmation resource guide in the back of the book where you can connect with the words that speak most strongly to you.

peep this . . .

Visualization is instrumental in your ability to manifest in this physical reality. What you "see" is what you get. The brain undergoes the same electrochemical processes when something is done in actuality or is imagined, so if you want to have an experience in the external world, first visualize it in the internal world.

Visualization is like a concentrated daydream. To visualize something is to see it in the mind's eye, to envision it. This is the basis for creating the reality you would like to see in real life. The important thing in visualization is to really *see* the details in your mind. As you are creating the picture in your mind engage all of the senses (smell that new car smell, hear the stereo bumpin' in your ears). The more real you imagine it the greater the results will be in life. This takes focus, which is like a laser beam that gives your intention extra power. Visualization is often used in conjunction with meditation to intensify an intention by including detail. Visualization may come easily for some and take practice for others. The same goes for focus and concentration. There are many exercises in this handbook where visualization techniques are used. The following are some ideas to sharpen one of your mental instruments, the mind's eye.

visualize this:

DECIDE ON SOMETHING simple to visualize: a banana, a tree, a rose, a car, whatever. Close your eyes and imagine the object you have chosen (sometimes it helps to imagine that there is a movie screen behind your closed eyelids and see the object on the screen). Take a few minutes to observe the object in your mind in as much detail as possible. Imagine what it feels like, smells like, sounds like, tastes like, etc. If your mind wanders, gently bring your attention back to the subject matter. After a few minutes open your eyes.

Write down as many details as you can remember in the space provided.

Was this simple or difficult for you? If you were not able to actually see the things in your mind, don't worry. Having the idea of the banana, or whatever, in your mind and thinking about the details is enough. The thought itself can still be effective with or without the picture. With practice and focus you will improve.

visualize this too:

CLOSE YOUR EYES and imagine/visualize that you are in a beautiful place. If you like, you can create a special place that you go in future meditations. It could be a tropical forest, a beach, an amazing house. Make it interesting, a secret door on the side of an old tree that leads down into a comfortable earthy room with a warm fireplace. Maybe you're on a cliff and can see for miles in every direction, eagles flying in the distance.

Notice things around you. What do you see? What can you touch, and how does it feel? What can you smell? What can you hear? Imagine as many details as you can.

When you are ready, open your eyes. Write down as many details here as you can remember. It may be helpful to write down the details you would like to "see" beforehand, and then do the visualization. Either way, it's *great!* You are well on your way to consciously creating your life!

I & I

"I and I is an expression to totalize the concept of one-ness, the oneness of two persons. God is within all of us and we're one people in fact. I and I means that God is in all men. The term is often used in place of 'you and I' or 'we' among Rastafarians, implying that both persons are united under the love of Jah."

—RASTAFARIAN SCHOLAR E. E. CASHMOR

what's the matter?
pg. 29

IF YOU LIVE in a city with a large West Indian population or have spent any time in the Caribbean islands you may be familiar with the term "I and I." The Rastafarian culture, which originated in Jamaica, uses the expression "I and I" instead of "you and I" or "we." This means I am I and you are I, everyone is I. This is a difficult concept to understand intellectually. How can billions of people be one? We have lived in these seemingly separate bodies for lifetimes. We identify ourselves and everything else with names. We live in a reality where everything is said to have an opposite.

Duality is something we experience on the level of form (in the physical realm); we communicate these polarities through language. Duality separates things from each other and ourselves. It says one thing is good and another is bad. Someone is nice and another is mean. With duality one thing cannot exist without its opposite. There would be no such thing as a short person if there weren't any tall people to compare them with. How could we know soft if we didn't know hard? This is why it is said that everything also exists in its opposite. (This is what the yin-yang symbol represents.) So in reality, dualism is a scale with which we compare the differences of a whole.

When we look at our world from a place of duality, everything seems separate from everything else. When we experience life with an awareness of wholeness, rather than the constant judgment created by duality, we'll feel a common bond with all life.

> **"You're soaking in it."** —MADGE

There is a oneness that permeates all life. People and everything in the world, the universe, the sun, a Hummer, a golf ball, are all manifested from the same vibrating energy substance. This is life energy, and it contains infinite potential. Life energy is a conscious, endless field that extends out forever in every direction. Life energy is but a manifestation of the Source, the spirit that resides in all life. Everything has a soul. Everything. We are endless. Man, matter, and everything in between (including the seemingly empty space) are completely, seamlessly connected. There is no way to separate yourself or anything else from it. You breathe it, eat it, wear it, smell it, hear it, do it, are it. Of course, your mind and perhaps your cirumstances may suggest otherwise. But this Source is our true self. So not only are *we* spiritual beings, *everything* is. All things seen and unseen come from the Source, are imbued throughout with Source energy, therefore are alive, and therefore are spiritual beings. This can be hard to relate to, especially in regards to inanimate objects. But yes, your toilet is a spiritual being. With this understanding, all of existence is spiritual in nature. It is not something that can actually be separated out from the rest of life. The idea that one is spiritual at church or when one prays, but is not spiritual when one is working or partying, does not make sense in these terms. You are life essence, Source, no matter who, what, or where you are and how you act. Giving attention to life as a spiritual experience makes miracles more obvious, makes the ethereal more palpable. We are not humans having a spiritual experience; we are spirits having a human experience.

Although you have only been in your body for a certain amount of time, and you may not remember anything prior to this life, your spirit has always lived. You are an immortal soul. You will live forever, not necessarily in this particular body. You will transcend this body, and at some point in your evolution you will likely have the ability to choose any type of physical manifestation. You are indestructible! You cannot be "done in." You cannot die or be killed. There will never be an end to you; you are infinite and eternal. Energy cannot be created or destroyed.

what's the matter?

There are many things that exist in the world of matter that people might say are not alive—rocks, a rubber tire, a pair of Nikes. But every scientist would agree that everything is alive on a molecular level. Everything is made of energy. Now we have all heard this, but truly realizing it is imperative to our spiritual evolution, as this understanding breaks down the barriers of separation.

Matter is energy in its slowest and densest form. When matter is broken down to its smallest measurable increment, we find the atom. Every type of matter in its simplest form is constructed of molecules made of atoms, whether it is the cells of a human heart, the bark of a tree, or the vinyl siding on a house. Even the seeming emptiness of space is full of molecules—carbon, oxygen, and so much more . . .

> "The Spirit is beyond sound and form, without touch and taste and perfume. It is eternal, unchangeable, and without beginning or end; indeed above reasoning. When consciousness of the Spirit manifests itself, man becomes free from the jaws of death."
>
> –*Upanishads* (c. 800 bce)

An atom is composed of a nucleus (the center of information), which is made up of protons and neutrons, and a corresponding number of electrons. The number of protons in the nucleus attracts to itself the same number of electrons, this creates an element. For example, an atom of aluminum has thirteen protons, and therefore thirteen electrons. The main difference between an atom of aluminum and an atom of oxygen (which has eight) is the number of protons, neutrons, and electrons that they each have. That's the only difference! Every atom in the whole of existence is comprised of exactly the same ingredients as every other atom. This concept is so simple, yet so profound. Atoms are amazing because they create what we know as matter, yet are not made of solid material—they are sparks of energy particles vibrating, dancing around each other. Science says that an atom is 99.999 percent empty space.

Another amazing discovery scientists have made is that electrons jump, or switch places with other electrons from different atoms. So all day long electrons from the atoms in the oxygen in the air you breathe exchange themselves with the electrons from the atoms in your lungs. Some of these electrons exchange with the blood, bones, and organs in your body. This exchange is always going on, inside of you and outside. Your skin is exchanging electrons with your clothes, which then exchange with the chair you're sitting on, et cetera. Human, plastic, or metal—everything is comprised of the same basic building block of life. This in itself is a wonderful example of the Oneness of all things. The universe and all of its contents are made of the exact same alive, conscious material.

Everything lives! Life energy saturates all that is, the seen and the unseen. Together they create the cosmic soup we call life. Truly absorbing and understanding this basic science is important. This life essence underlies everything we can experience with or without our senses. This energy, this oneness, permeates all of infinity. It is what everything is made of inside and out. You can't escape it; if you try to run and hide, you'll just be hiding in it. It fills every seeming empty space. There is no place that this energy is not. It is this life energy that we, by use of our mind, utilize to create our constant reality whether or not we are conscious of it. The more we reflect upon and begin to truly understand this, the more powerful we become as we begin to use the infinite potential and knowledge we have access to.

oneness meditation

This exercise is good to do lying down on the floor, but sitting or standing is fine too.

GROUND YOURSELF; use the foundation meditation or any other process to bring yourself to a centered place. Focus on your breathing for several breaths until you feel you are ready.

As you inhale, imagine that a field of golden light surrounds you. Every time you inhale, imagine that this field expands several feet. Visualize that your feet grow roots and that these roots grow into the ground and spread out. Imagine that who you are doesn't stop at your skin, be formless. Continue to expand your golden field with your breaths until it encompasses your home, your city, and eventually the world. Realize that although you have expanded your essence to include the whole world you have not lost your sense of uniqueness. Feel affinity and compassion for all things and people in the world. Realize there is no separation from you and the Creator of all things seen and unseen. Your awareness is expanding, allowing you to embrace the whole universe, the oneness of all.

Give thanks to life for this experience and when you are ready, bring your attention back to your body. Follow the breath in and out, feel your body. Slowly and when you are ready, open your eyes.

THE JOURNEY IN

THERE ARE SO MANY cool things about urban living. Career and business opportunities abound. Great nightlife, famous sports teams. Most cities boast a large selection of restaurants featuring flavors from all over the world. City dwellers are the first to get wind of new trends in style and fashion. It is easy to get caught up in the frenzy of the urban experience; many of us have big city dreams about fast cars and fat pockets. But if you really stopped for a moment and took a good long look at what is really important to you, where would love be on your list? Most of what we are up to in life is a roundabout, even ass backwards way of trying to get love. Have you ever said, "If I could just get _____ (fill in the blank) I would be happy"? We are looking for a level of satisfaction that seems somehow to be just out of reach. When we feel incomplete, getting and having the high-paying job, the fresh ride, the fashion, is all about attaining that fleeting feeling of satisfaction. Trying to fill ourselves up with something, anything, so that we might feel whole, if only for a moment. The satisfaction is fleeting because we are looking for it in the wrong place. You can never find it outside of yourself. It doesn't exist there. It is love we want, to have and to give. But if we don't realize it we will spend our life chasing things, trying to fill ourselves up with this unobtainable satisfaction.

Sure, it's great to have money, a gorgeous girlfriend or boyfriend, and the home of your dreams. But we also deserve to live a life full of meaning, full of love. To affect your external reality in a profound and lasting way you must first tune into your inner self. This means becoming aware of what is going on inside you, inside your heart and your mind. When you have inner harmony, genuine love, and acceptance for yourself, you create harmony in every aspect of your life. The desperate feeling that you must get! get! get! quiets down. When you learn to honor and love yourself and others just as they are, you have found the priceless jewel of your own being. You are whole; nothing outside of you can complete you. You are complete unto yourself. Accepting this idea isn't always easy. We have been trained, and quite well, to see our personal power as being very limited. As the truth begins to dawn upon you, and you decide to embrace your divinity, the universe dances with joy. This is when life really gets fun. Without the frantic feeling of emptiness and lack, the things that you once chased come easily to you.

How, in our busy lives, do we sync our rhythms with those of the infinite universe? The answer seems so simple: with love and with gratitude. It *seems* simple. We have been taught many things by authority figures, but one thing that hasn't always been nurtured or encouraged is how to love ourselves. We have been taught to be selfless, to work hard for others. But rarely are we encouraged to honor our true feelings, to take time and give love to ourselves. When you have a healthy appreciation for yourself you complete the cycle of love within yourself. You give yourself love and receive love from yourself. You honor your divine and powerful self. You can then create an intimate relationship, a delicious love affair with yourself, and all of life. When you are deeply in love with your *whole* self, the *whole* world opens up to you and falls deeply in love with you. In truth all of creation has always been in love with you. You just couldn't see it through the cloud of judgments you have about yourself and others. You couldn't see through the walls you built to protect yourself from all the hurt you've experienced, and are now hell bent on trying to avoid.

• •

What does it really mean to love yourself, and what does it feel like? How do you know if you are even doing it right? Loving yourself means accepting you as you are without judgment. And if you find yourself being judgmental, not judging that. It is appreciation for the great universe in all its limitless manifestations because everything is God or the Source. Self-love is the path to self-awareness, mindfulness, and enlightenment. When we truly accept ourselves, we open ourselves to greater possibility, for it is our beliefs about ourselves that create our reality. Your relationship with yourself is the reflection you see in the world. Everything you will experience in this life is a direct reflection of the relationship you have with yourself, everything. When we are in balance, we experience outer harmony. If we want to experience abundance, joy, and love in our circumstances, we must nurture those qualities within us so our outer lives will fall into alignment.

How do you relate to yourself? With patience and compassion or anger and disappointment? Are you at peace with mistakes that you've made in the past, or do you still feel shameful or embarrassed? Are you confident, shy, fearful? Do you have issues about your self-esteem? Consider your personality and reflect upon your life and how situations that you encounter are results of how you feel about yourself.

Warriors, in this magical process we will discover our magnificent selves, our whole selves. There are countless ways to nurture, appreciate, accept, and ultimately love ourselves. It begins with an awareness of the thought process . . .

elevate your mental

Your experience is unique to you. Your understanding and the way you perceive things, no matter what they are, will be different from everyone else's, simply because of your unique, individual experience. The thoughts that come to your mind first move through the tons of information that you've gathered as you've lived your life. Your DNA is encoded with genetic information and, some say, memories of past lives. Everything that you have experienced is filed away somewhere in the subconscious mind, whether you remember it or not.

When you have a thought or experience, your mind references it against your past thoughts and experiences. This produces an automatic response system from which life is created on autopilot; everything is based on past occurrences, shaping your present moment from your personal history. This is why many people feel stuck; stuck (did I say stuck) in their job, relationship, or attitude. This automatic response system can work in your favor when your thought process is referencing loving and empowering thoughts and memories. Later chapters feature exercises to retrain your thinking patterns.

Who and where you are right now in this exact moment is a product of your past thoughts, feelings, and actions. What you experience in the next moment, tomorrow, and next year, will be a product of how you are feeling, what you are thinking, and what action you are taking right *now*. Being aware means being conscious of your present moment, realizing that right now you are creating your current reality, and that of the next moment.

The lives we are living are reflections of whatever we think about most, as well as our deeply held beliefs. The majority of people are unconscious about this connection between our thoughts and our realities. When we are unconscious of our thought processes and belief systems we often create unhappy scenarios or lives. It is important to really understand that like it or not, you are responsible for your life. This one point is the hardest for many of us to accept. Our society promotes victim consciousness (this is why lawyers get paid so much), which creates an environment of blame where no one is responsible for his or her own life or conditions. Crazy and sometimes terrible things happen that we cannot control, but you have a choice about how you will react to them, and how you will let them affect you. Mourn the things that must be mourned, and then release. Take a moment right now to gauge your feelings and reaction to what you just read. Notice if you are feeling resistance or anger to the idea that we are responsible for our situations. If so, this is your ego talking. If you choose to take responsibility for your life your ego will no longer be able to identify itself as a victim. The ego loves being a victim because it gets so much attention from others, which feeds it. People who believe themselves to be victims also complain a lot. Complaining usually makes one person or group the bad guy, and the complainer the victim. This attitude makes it hard to break through mental boundaries that keep you in stuck mode. Blaming others or society for the way your life is creates mental chaos. If there is chaos in the mind, there is likely to be chaos of some form in your life. This is a disempowering way to live. And as long as a person chooses to see themselves as a victim of their experience or environment, they will likely be unable to consciously create their reality. This is not to say that you need to blame yourself for the unhappy things that have happened to you; this is not about who is to blame for what has happened in the past. Blame creates guilt, which is a very heavy and often unhealthy emotion. The past is gone, let it lie. Decide, here and now, to take responsibility for your life.

It's time to consciously take on the proper thought patterns to balance our lives. We all deserve to live, love, and flourish. We can become no better than the thoughts we have, and the actions we take. Allow yourselves to have divine, compassionate, and abundant thoughts. These powerful thought vibrations couldn't help but manifest blessed states of being into your/our waking reality. Learning to shift your awareness to accepting that you are the creator of your life is the first step to understanding and using your great power. Soul Warriors accept, embrace, and live from the perspective that they are responsible for and have the power to create their reality. Rather than seeing this as a depressing or limiting idea, you can use it to discover a deep power and freedom within.

mind chatter . . .

In order to consciously create our lives we must first become aware of our unconscious thought patterns. Our minds chatter incessantly all day long, judging ourselves and everything we come in contact with. Change and growth scare the hell out of many of us. We internalize this fear and the mind takes over, wanting to protect us from "the world out there." The mind often talks us of out of doing the things that will bring us the most joy and growth. The changes that life brings us contain gifts of understanding and continuous opportunities to experience the flow of love.

WARRIOR WORKSHEET

Identify the type of thought patterns you are currently having about your life. Write down all the thoughts and words that come to you regarding the following categories.

WORK

RELATIONSHIPS

MONEY

LOVE

PHYSICAL BODY/HEALTH

MIND

VACATION/PERSONAL TIME

SPIRIT

Reflect on these aspects in your own life and see if the circumstances you are currently experiencing are reflecting the words you wrote for each category.

Go back to each category and identify the language that is supportive or positive.

Then identify the language and specific words that are negative or unsupportive.

Repeat the exercise using descriptive words you would like to associate and experience in your life in regards to each category.

WORK

RELATIONSHIPS

MONEY

LOVE

PHYSICAL BODY/HEALTH

MIND

SPIRIT

Becoming aware of our thought patterns is the first real step in creating the changes we want to see in our lives. It is these thought patterns that are creating the template of our internal and external experience, most often without our conscious attention or our permission. If we are constantly talking down to ourselves or we don't allow ourselves to believe in love and beauty, we may never experience true joy.

A single thought alone has infinite power. When we have the same type of thought over and over it creates its own groove in our energy body. Once we have created a thought groove (be it an empowering or disempowering thought), a thought pattern has been created. This makes it easier for the thought to move through the mind; there is little or no resistance to the thought. This is also called the law of inertia. The law of inertia states, "An object at rest tends to stay at rest and an object in motion tends to stay in motion with the same speed and in the same direction unless acted upon by an unbalanced force." Once inertia has begun, a certain thought pattern needs little or no attention to manifest its reflection in our external state or attitude. For example, if you have regular thoughts such as "I can't afford it" or "it's too expensive" or "there's never enough money," you are creating a broke lifestyle groove or thought pattern in your mind/body that in turn is attracting the exact circumstances you are thinking about. This holds true for any repetitious thought or deeply held belief. We all have deeply embedded thought forms about who we believe we are. These beliefs play themselves out in our everyday lives. The doubts and judgments we have about ourselves become the experiences we ultimately have every day; we give so much attention to the stuff that we don't want or like, we attract it by default. What would happen if we could accept ourselves just as we are, and run a stream of unconditional love through our hearts?

collective consciousness

At every moment what we *think,* feel, and believe matters and what we do with those thoughts matters, not only to you and those most immediately around you, but to the entire universe. The vibration you are resonating moves endlessly into the collective consciousness. As we are all connected to each other, we are all affected by each other. Warriors, by being in alignment with love and gratitude we raise the vibration of the entire universe. It all begins with you. If you want to change the world, love yourself. Through an authentic love of yourself you can effectively contribute to the healing of the collective consciousness. Ask yourself, what kind of impact are your thoughts, feelings, and actions having on the world?

MONSTERS IN THE CLOSET

MONSTERS, SKELETONS—we all got 'em hiding deep in the corners of our closets. Ugly little things we have pushed below the surface of our everyday life; things we have done that we are ashamed of, parts of ourselves that we don't like, scary things we are afraid think about. But guess what? There are precious jewels in there too. Get out the flashlights—we're going diamond mining.

The work in this chapter is in-depth and needs your time and attention. Set some time aside for yourself when you know you will not be interrupted. Do the exercises at a pace that allows the fullness of each one to affect you. These Warrior Worksheets are designed to find parts of you that you have consciously and unconsciously disowned. It won't be easy, but if you work through these processes, you will illuminate the darkness with the light of your very being. You will discover your whole self.

ego shmego

As stated before, you are not just your body or your mind; these are the vehicle of the spirit that is your true self. That being said, you are also not your feelings, your fears, your hopes, or dreams. The ego likes to identify feelings and things with itself. This is how it creates an identity. The ego gets very attached to its identity, and it doesn't have to be a positive one. The ego doesn't care if its identity is one of suffering and victimization or that of a parent or a spiritual leader. It does not care; it just needs an identity to survive.

The voice or voices that you hear incessantly talking in your head are the ego at work. You are not these voices. You aren't angry, tired, or sleepy. The true you observes these states of being. Spiritual transformation is the process of disentangling yourself from the power of the ego. The ego identifies with belief systems, ailments, politics, religions, ideals, morals, and many other things that will give it an identity to attach to. As you uncover your fears, judgments, and shadows you realize your wholeness, and the ego loses power.

The ego is also a tool; it is an instrument for the liberation of the mind and spirit. The ego sets forth to bind the mind with it's ideas and rules. It allows you to see ideas that do not serve you or humanity by exposing those parts that are not healed or not in alignment with wholeness. We can use the ego as a map to point us in the direction of that which needs the most love and attention.

What are some of the ways your ego controls the way you experience life? If you are not sure yet, go on to the next section.

scaredy cat?

Our society is run by a government, corporations, and religious institutions that are very aware of the power of fear. It is used as a tool to keep people under control, to keep us from knowing that we are powerful beings. We believe in the monsters that have been created to scare us away from ourselves. We hide them deep within, and then make every effort to pretend they aren't there. We then respond to the world out of fear and the illusion of lack, which is reflected to us in return. If we experience fear and lack it is because these are beliefs we hold about ourselves.

> **"I learned that courage was not the absence of fear, but the triumph over it. The brave man is not he who does not feel afraid, but he who conquers that fear."**
>
> **—NELSON MANDELA**

Fear is driven into us by every media outlet we can imagine, trying to pull us in every direction so that they can have their way with our money, our minds, and our bodies. We fear that we are not beautiful enough, that we are ugly, too fat, or too skinny. We fear that we are too angry, too nice, too soft, or too hard. We fear that we are too loud, or too shy, or not successful enough, that we are unworthy, unlovable. We are bombarded by ads to lose weight, to get Botox, to get life insurance. Every evening the majority of Americans invite fear and violence into their home, and call it entertainment. We can turn to any channel and watch children be brutalized, or watch men and women beat and kill each other. The news channels show the atrocities that are happening worldwide. We internalize all of these things and think this is the reality we are living in. We then go out into the world fearful of all the things that can happen to us at any second, never realizing that these fearful vibrations we fill ourselves with daily attract more terrible things and more fear into our lives. What if our children didn't watch people kill each other in their own home, on the television? What would our world be like?

The choice to live in fear is just that, a choice. The ego identifies with these fears and creates a fearful personality. As you begin to connect with your infinite self you will naturally begin to free yourself from the chains of fear. You may still occasionally feel the emotion of fear, but you will not be driven and controlled by it. Of course, fear has its benefits—as an instinct, it can save your life. But here we are speaking of the undercurrent of fear that is part of our reality on a moment-to-moment basis, so much so that we are barely aware of it.

All situations and emotions we can experience here have been placed before us for our benefit and growth, and this includes fear. It is a learning tool, an opportunity to wake up to our true unlimited self. Fear is an emotion, an expression like any other. When we acknowledge it as just another expression of life it will flow out of us, and we will not be crippled by its grip. As with everything else, we are not to judge it, but accept that it exists. It cannot disempower us if it is not repressed or avoided. This does not mean you allow fear to take you over, either. It means simply acknowledge your fears. Do not be afraid to admit that you are afraid of whatever it is. We fear our fears, often because we don't really know what they are. You are not your emotions, therefore you are not your fear. It is when fear is denied that it is dangerous. Pretending we don't have emotions is what makes them more powerful. Nothing likes to be denied; pushing something away makes it try harder to get your attention. When you look at your fear as another manifestation of the Source, therefore of yourself, you realize there is nothing to be afraid of. Basically it is through fear that fearful things are created. Fear, as a product of the mind, cannot be rationalized away by the mind, but it can be liberated or transformed.

There are several productive ways to deal with the emotion of fear, to release or transmute it.

WARRIOR WORKSHEET

Are you afraid that you will be alone? Afraid of death? Afraid that you are not smart enough? In the space below make a list of a few fears you have, whatever they may be. Acknowledge your fears, pull them out of the closet, hang them up and look at them. Allow yourself to feel whatever comes up with each fear. Write a little about each fear, about why you are afraid of these things. There is no right or wrong way to do this exercise. Fear projects a negative outcome onto a future that we can't actually know.

The following are three ideas to help you balance the energy of fear.

Close your eyes and for a moment allow yourself to feel the fear that is attached to each of the things you have written. It is amazing how powerful the feeling becomes; it can even become an intense and overwhelming feeling of panic. Notice the power that fear can potentially have over your life. Now imagine a cord attached to the root of your spine and visualize all of your fears funneling down into this cord, and this energy being recycled by the Earth. Fill yourself up with love and light.

When you have considered why each of these things brings you fear, take a moment to love the part of you that is afraid. Imagine that this part of you is a frightened child and offer it your love.

Close your eyes and allow the feeling of fear that you have attached to the above issues come up in you. Visualize it as a grey energy swirling around you. Now visualize a stream of golden liquid light entering through the top of your head and coming out of your heart. This golden liquid light fills all of the space around you and dissolves all of the grey energy.

When we acknowledge our fears, their power over us dissipates. They may still exist on some level, but you cannot be unconsciously controlled by them if you know what they are.

the judge

Existence and all its limitless possibilities are within you always, within your reach, if only you *allow it to be.* We have a tendency to diminish ourselves with judgment. People can be so hard on them-selves, so unforgiving. Judgment inhibits the manifestation of our deepest desires. Sometimes within the scheme of things our little lives seem small and we may feel ineffective or insignificant. Ideas of what we can or can't do have been thrust upon us through our parents, teachers, and society's limited view and understanding of reality. In truth, you are infinite potential; there is no true limitation except where you perceive it. You can only really experience what you can believe and conceive. If you desire to experience things beyond what you already think you know, be willing to open yourself up, and to expand past your current limitations.

Life on Earth is a spiritual school and playground. In this sense, there is no good or bad, only what is. There are so many fantastic differences in the human race, and they make us unique and wonderful. Many of us were not brought up to appreciate our differences. We make one difference good or acceptable and another bad or unacceptable. When doing this, we are giving more value to one thing and less to another. As we become more self-aware we begin to understand that these differences are parts of a whole. Your true self *is* whole, it consists of all parts, even the parts we are afraid of, the parts we don't like about ourselves. By experiencing these polarities, we transform and remember who we really are.

● ●

Every time we make a judgment about anything or anyone else we are telling a story about ourself. If we say that someone is ugly, we may have learned that we wouldn't be loved if we were considered ugly. If we say someone is evil, we may have been taught that some people are better than others, or maybe we are expressing our fear of God and his wrath. Every judgment about yourself and others is a reflection of fear that you have about yourself. It is a mechanism to separate you from everyone else. When you judge something you are creating a separation between you and it, or between it and something else. There is no true separation except where you perceive it. Everything comes from the same divine Source; this means that each person has just as much value as anyone else. Each person has come here to learn their own lessons, to gain their own understanding through their trials and tribulations, through their joys and sorrows. It is not for you to judge another. All judgment of the outside world comes from judgment of the self.

> **"Cradle your wounded places like precious babies."**
>
> **—SARK**

This is not to say that one should not have preferences. Preference is not the same as judgment. You may prefer summer to winter, apples to peaches. Does this diminish the value of winter or peaches? No, it is merely preference. While loving and appreciating all things as equal, you prefer apples. This is the release from judgment.

There is a common judgment in our society that thin is better than fat. Fat is an expression of life that is just as valid as thin. But thin gets more value from our society. There are societies that value heavier people, and thinner people are undervalued, this too is out of balance. If we fear fat we create fat, or we create a life in fear of fat that is filled with self imposed limitation. If we are in harmony with our bodies, we are naturally attracted to healthy things that align with that harmony. We don't judge ourselves when we eat things we enjoy because we are not in fear of these things.

Every time we have a harsh judgment about ourselves we are exposing a wounded place. Take a moment to love the disillusioned child in you who believes it is not good enough. Cradle that part of you, or the part that was shunned or abused by others who had their own issues and wounded places. Cradle it like an innocent baby.

We all have the tendency to make judgments about ourselves and others. The ego enjoys making judgments because its identity is tied up in the beliefs created by these judgments. The key is to notice when you are judging something and then say gently to yourself, "Thank you for sharing." When you find yourself being judgmental, do not devalue yourself; don't judge yourself for judging. It is no more healthy to say, "bad girl, don't judge!" than it is to judge in the first place. Observe the judge, which is an element of your ego, without giving it any power or trying to repress it. Just notice and release. After a while the judge quiets down when it doesn't get the constant attention it is used to.

● ●

Try this technique to quiet the judge: say, " . . . and beautiful" or ". . . and divine" or " . . . with love" when you catch the mind making a judgment. For example: "He sure is fat, and beautiful." "They are so evil, and wonderful." "I am such a bitch, and divine." "What a jerk, with love."

These are judgments also, but they live in love, and they will lighten the mood, often making you laugh to think them or say them out loud. A judgment is nothing more than a thought expressing itself—see it as it is. You have a choice in how you respond to it. Observe it and release it, then choose a preference of nonjudgment. As we learn to be gentle and loving with ourselves, we learn to not judge ourselves. We then automatically become less judgmental of others and the world.

* * *

WARRIOR WORKSHEET

What are some of the most common things that you judge? About yourself, about others? Write a list about common things you dislike or disapprove of.

Write down a few things you like or approve of. Notice whether or not this is a preference or a judgment. A judgment gives more value to the things you approve of.

FOR EXAMPLE:

This is the only good song on the whole CD (judgment = the rest of the CDE is crap), or *The whole CD is great, but this song is my favorite* (preference).

guilty as charged

Forgiveness is one of the major tools of transformation. We hold onto the anger and disappointment towards others for so long, we often forget that deep down we are still upset about something. An issue never got resolved within us and therefore is still affecting us in ways we are likely not aware of. The ego likes to hold grudges so that it can feel that it is better than someone else. When someone hurts your feelings or angers you and you choose to hold onto resentment it is you who is hurting yourself, not them. Resentment and lack of forgiveness give the ego more power. Yes, maybe someone said or did something selfish and it really hurt you. Shame on them. But every time you think about it, every time you relive it, you hurt yourself again. Every time you think, "What an asshole!" and still have anger about that person, you are hurting yourself. The energy we send out into the universe will always come back to us. When you judge another, you judge yourself.

Self-forgiveness is even more important. The guilt we have stored up throughout our lives for the countless things we may have done that has upset, angered, or hurt other people can live forever if we hold on to it. Guilt can be a monkey on your back till the day you die, and beyond. We all screw up and do and say things we wish we hadn't. You are responsible for ill deeds that you have done. The other person is responsible for the way they choose to feel (internalize) about it. Everyone is responsible for their own feelings. It is up to you to forgive yourself, to release yourself from memories and guilt for things you have done in the past. There is nothing that cannot be forgiven. Forgive yourself, even and especially if the person has yet to forgive you. You do not deserve to suffer for the rest of your life because you screwed up at some point. Accept what you have done and realize that, yes, it might have hurt someone. That person asked for that lesson as much as you did, consciously or not. Forgive yourself, forgive everyone, and forgive even the people you think are the scum of the earth. Who made you the judge? Can you imagine how much lighter you would be if you could forgive people and release your judgment of them?

Forgiveness is a form of acceptance. You have a choice to accept that something hurtful has happened: you can choose to feel the emotions that come up around the issue, and release. This is forgiveness. Or you can choose to hold onto the pain until it manifests itself as illness or more anger. Once something bad has happened, whatever it is, you might as well accept it. Not accepting it does not change the fact that it happened. But forgiveness of self and others can heal our hearts and make room for love.

> **"Whenever you accept what is, something deeper emerges than what is. So, you can be trapped in the most painful dilemma, external or internal, the most painful feelings or situation, and the moment you accept what is, you go beyond it, you transcend it. Even if you feel hatred, the moment you accept that this is what you feel, you transcend it. It may still be there, but suddenly you are at a deeper place where it doesn't matter that much anymore."**
>
> **—ECKHART TOLLE**

WARRIOR WORKSHEET

Take a few minutes to think about people who you feel have wronged you in some way. Have you forgiven them? Do they think you have forgiven them, but you still feel angry or upset about it? Write statements describing any events that happened where you feel you were hurt by another's actions. Next to each statement describe the feeling associated with each of these experiences. If you feel emotional about these things allow yourself to feel the emotion. Allow the anger and the tears. This is a chance to release, so don't hold back. *(If you need more room use blank pages in the center of the book.)*

When you have had enough time to sufficiently feel whatever comes up regarding each of the above statements, make a decision to forgive. Write a statement of forgiveness.

Reflect upon things you feel guilty about or ashamed of that you have not forgiven yourself for, things that have occurred that you have not made peace with. This may be painful, yet to realize your wholeness it is very necessary. It is crucial to let yourself feel any and all emotions that are tied up in these memories. Write these things down.

When you are ready, decide you are ready to forgive yourself, ready to stop punishing yourself for the past. You have grown from your mistakes and you deserve to be free! Write statements of self-forgiveness.

If you feel you can, apologize to those you have hurt. You are not responsible for the feelings of others, but sometimes when you acknowledge the past you can help them heal too.

If you feel that writing statements of forgiveness is not sufficient to activate a true release or real feeling of forgiveness, do the foundation meditation from Chapter Two. During this meditation imagine that you are forgiving either yourself or another person. Then release the issue down the cord into the Earth to be recycled. You may want to do this a few times. Fill yourself with light.

You may find that there are still remnants of guilty feelings or other emotions still hanging around after you have done either the writing exercise or the meditation. These emotional wounds are usualy quite deep. If so, you may want to repeat this exercise every night for a week.

shadows on the inside

We all have facets of ourselves that we don't like. Maybe you are ashamed of them, or even fearful. The famous psychologist Carl Jung called these aspects our shadows. These shadows can be traits that we describe as bad or good, but what makes them shadows is that they are denied or repressed. We have hidden our shadows deeply within our consciousness, and to some degree we believe that if our shadows are exposed, everyone will know that there is something wrong with us, and that we are not worthy of love.

Many of us subconsciously believe that if we look deep enough, if we dig out this old crap, that we will find something terrible. So we fear ourselves: we fear all of these things that we have pushed away for so long. But

Shad-ow, *noun:* hidden or unconscious aspects of oneself, both good and bad, which the ego has either repressed or never realized; rejected aspects of ourselves and undeveloped potential.

just because we have pushed it away doesn't mean it's dead and buried. No, what happens is that we project this fear onto the world, onto our loved ones and strangers.

> "The psychological rule says that when an inner situation is not made conscious, it happens outside as fate. That is to say, when the individual remains undivided and does not become conscious of his inner opposite, the world must act out the conflict and be torn into opposing halves."
> —CARL JUNG

The truth is, in order for us to be whole, fulfilled beings we must embrace our whole selves. Jung also believed that 90 percent of our shadows are gold. When we can accept all of ourselves, we find our gold, our wholeness. There are positives in these denied parts of ourselves. There are good parts about our bad parts.

Much of what we experience in the outside world is a reflection of the judgments we hold about ourselves. These judgments are simply limitations or fears we have created about ourselves. We think we are wrong or bad for having certain ideas or feelings.

For example, it is not "wrong" to be angry. Anger is just like any other emotion; it just wants to be felt, acknowledged, and accepted. When it is judged or pushed away, it grows in order to get your attention, and sooner or later it blows. If one could feel angry without judging it as something to be ashamed of, the feeling would quickly dissipate. There are a whole host of thoughts swimming around that some may consider immoral. So what?! They are just thoughts. If you have a thought, whatever it is, and you judge yourself as wrong or bad for having had the thought, you have devalued the thought and you add it to your pile of shadows. You may then feel guilty about having these "bad" thoughts. This guilty energy may in turn create or attract the "bad" circumstances in your external reality. When you can have thoughts and let them be, let them flow in and out of you without guilt and judgment, you will not be driven by an unconscious need to actually carry out the ideas that you would prefer not to experience.

> "If you wish to manifest your full potential you have to reclaim the parts of yourself that you've denied, hidden, or given away to others." —DEBBIE FORD

Our shadows are gifts. They are opportunities to integrate polarities, the separation within you. There is no part of us that is unacceptable or unlovable. We make those distinctions with our ego mind. The shadows in us continue to grow and fester because they want to be loved just like the rest of us. We continue to resist these parts of ourselves, but what you resist persists.

This process is about understanding that we are all One, meaning we all have the capacity to exhibit any and all human characteristics. We judge these characteristics as good and bad, but in truth they are all parts of a whole. These shadows are not our true self, only aspects of the ego. To embrace our wholeness, we must acknowledge these traits, honor them, and see how they have contributed to our lives. And if they have yet to contribute, then see how they could contribute one day. How can we use these seemingly negative aspects and integrate them? When we accept all parts of ourselves, the parts we were afraid of lose their power, and they can then accent our personality instead of controlling it. We don't grow from ridding ourselves from the darkness (which is impossible anyway); the darkness is an integral part of our lives. We grow by bringing consciousness to our darkness. People are afraid to confront these shadows because they fear the pain they will cause. But in this darkness you will find the gold and diamonds of joy and fulfillment because you embrace and love your whole self, your authentic self. To embrace a shadow is to love it, and allow it to coexist with all your other qualities. Find the gift each shadow brings, view it with compassion and see its innocence. To be divine is to be whole, and this means to include all, the positive and the negative.

> **"My being is no imposition upon life. What liberation!"**
>
> **—IMURI**

it takes one to know one

People most often judge others when they display qualities that the person cannot accept in themself. This is called projection. We are all, in effect, mirrors for each other. We have become experts at hiding our shadows from ourselves, and without projection we might not find them. When one sees fault in another it is often because he or she also has this fault but refuses to see it. We judge someone for something we have done, or something that under the right circumstances we are capable of doing.

We hide our wonderful aspects, too. Many of us have hidden away the powerful parts of ourselves, and those too are shadows. If we see beautiful things in another person, and worship this person for having these wonderful traits, it is likely that we share these traits but have pushed them into our shadows. Are you an artist, but have denied your creativity? Do you have the gift of eloquence and the ability to move people with your words, but are too shy to talk to people? Are you beautiful, but hide your beauty because you were taught that beauty is vanity and sinful? When we admire something in someone it is an opportunity to retrieve those parts of ourselves. Think about people in your life or other figures that you admire. Consider what it is about them that you appreciate. Can you also see that trait in yourself? If not, then you have just met a shadow. You are only able to see in others the traits that you also share; maybe not in the exact form as the other, but to some degree. Embrace it, claim it, for it is yours.

When there is a part of our self that we are keeping repressed it is not unusual to attract people into our lives that have these characteristics. This is a gift of the universe to help us embrace our whole self by revealing to us who we are and the parts of ourselves that we are in denial of.

There are many valuable things formed and found deep in the dark. Seeds sprout and grow in the dark; the dark is essential. It is not for us to hide from the dark but to go into the dark, to dig out our diamonds, and to water our precious seeds.

The following exercises are inspired by *The Dark Side of the Light Chasers* by Debbie Ford.

WARRIOR WORKSHEET

Answer these questions as truthfully as you can.

What am I afraid I or someone else might find out about me?

How have I lied to myself or others?

_____

_____

What parts of my life would I like to transform?

_____

_____

Write a list of types of people or specific people you disapprove of. Then define which traits you dislike about these people.

FOR EXAMPLE:

some politicians   *TRAITS = sneaky, ruthless, liar*

Make a list of the types of people or specific people you like and admire. Then define which traits you like about these people.

FOR EXAMPLE:

Mother Theresa   *TRAITS = compassionate, selfless*

All of the traits you have listed above are parts of your ego, some hidden, some not so hidden. Some you already knew about, others you can't see how they relate to you at all. We are all one. The potential of all humankind exists in you.

Own each of these traits, positive and negative, by taking them one at a time and saying, "Sometimes I feel _____." If there is one that is particularly hard for you to honor, say it in front of a mirror repeatedly until you are no longer affected by it.

Honor Your Shadows . . .

The following is a list of negative traits. As you read them circle any that you dislike or that really catch your attention. Circle any you know are shadows.

uncaring	hostile	ungrateful	phony
distant	unsure	unappreciative	wimpy
cold	unenthusiastic	lazy	evil
aloof	apathetic	dishonest	alcoholic
unmotivated	indifferent	egocentric	manipulative
rejecting	inflexible	conceited	ugly
closed	rigid	pessimistic	fat
guarded	unbending	insecure	stupid
secretive	scattered	late	desperate
unfeeling	authoritarian	naïve	childish
callous	angry	impractical	perverted
intractable	depressed	undisciplined	easy
hectic	unforgiving	dependent	sneaky
cheerless	resentful	narrow	critical
gloomy	spiteful	suspicious	prejudiced
grumpy	unfocused	mistrusting	bossy
inconsiderate	small-minded	pretentious	cheating
uncooperative	miserly	unreliable	mooching
indecisive	selfish	disrespectful	intolerant
unhelpful	controlling	rude	freaky
combative	hostile	impolite	idiotic
sour	unfriendly	indifferent	empty
cowering	wasteful	complacent	ridiculous
fearful	cheap	jealous	trashy
closed	stingy	envious	slutty
stubborn	arrogant	cruel	old
whiney	deceiving	mean	scary
impolite	malicious	immature	frail
uncommitted	hateful	vain	

Add any characteristics that may be missing.

Now, take each word that you circled, and one by one say "Sometimes I feel_____." It is not unusual to have an emotional reaction during this process. These shadows are highly charged and have been avoided at all costs for a long time. Welcome your tears or any other emotion; you are releasing toxins that have been stored in your body and subconscious. If you find it is hard to honor certain words and traits, stand in front of the mirror and say them over and over until they no longer distress you.

Whew! You did it! You have faced your demons and are still alive to talk about it! How do you feel? It is not unusual to feel emotionally drained, especially if there were heavy emotions expressed during your process. It took a lot of energy to hold those shadows down for so long. Rejoice in the integration of your scattered parts. You are becoming aware of yourself as a whole being. This calls for celebration! Really, find a way to appreciate yourself. Rest. Journal. Put on an uplifting movie. Relax. Take a bath, pour yourself a glass of wine, or give yourself a big hug. You deserve it!

If you still feel emotional, sad, or angry after the process, consider doing some more reflecting and accepting of your shadows. Over the next few days pay close attention to your feelings, judgments, and dreams. Now that you have embraced many of your shadows, there may be more undiscovered shadows that float to the surface of your attention. You have let up most of the pressure used to repress your shadows and so they will likely take advantage of the situation. They just want to be loved. Own each one as it unfolds, it becomes easier and easier.

Write about this process too, if you feel inspired.

THE CARING AND FEEDING OF SOULS

WE ARE about to start getting real juicy. It is time now to turn your attention to loving, nurturing, and enjoying your self. This section is full of ideas, rituals, and meditations to add joy to your experience, creating an appreciation of your self as a divine and magnificent being.

oasis in the city

Your home is your oasis: it is where you go to rejuvenate, relax, and get away from the world out there. We want our homes to be the place where the weight of the world melts off of us, a place where we can give to ourselves and receive those gifts. When you are focusing on nurturing yourself, it is really wonderful to have a sacred space within your home. If you live alone, you could

[
TIP:
Sage or smudge sticks have been used for centuries by the indigenous peoples of the Americas in rituals for purification and cleansing. To use: hold a flame to the thick end of the smudge stick until an ember forms. Wave the stick around in the area you would like to cleanse, be it a room, a person, or yourself. Soft blowing on the ember will keep it lit. Set it in a metal bowl or some other burn-proof vessel. The ember will usually burn out by itself, or use a few drops of water to put it out.
]

consider your whole home your sacred space, but it helps to have a particular area where you concentrate your intentions and practice. If you have a family or housemates, carve out a little niche, a special space for yourself, in your bedroom or a large closet. It is in this space that you feel safe, and where you can be alone without distractions even if only for a few minutes at a time.

Your sacred space is where you go when you have a moment to meditate, journal, exercise, or do yoga. It is where you attend to yourself, where you do your soul work, your warrior work. Make it as welcoming as you can, whatever that means to you. Perhaps add big floor pillows or a fluffy rug to sit on. Plants bring good vibrations to any space, as well as fresh air. Lighting is also important; a favorite lamp and full-spectrum light bulbs can bring some great light into your area. Candles are highly recommended—they create a wonderful ambiance, and dancing fire energy accents any sacred space. Hang pictures of things that make you feel good. Keep colored pens and a journal there for writing, drawing, or doodling. Burn incense or sage when you are going to meditate, or to clear the space of stagnant energy. If there are children or others in your home, set boundaries about who can and cannot be in this space.

Enjoy the silence when relaxing in your space or listen to soft music with earphones if you need to shut out other sounds. Use this space for reading or to enjoy a cup of tea. Come to this space as often as you can, even if it is just long enough to say a prayer, mantra, or affirmation.

Of course, many of us city apartment dwellers don't have enough room to create a fixed sacred space. No worries—create an oasis-to-go. Fill a basket or tub with items for a sacred space on the move. Include items like a small pillow, candles, incense, sacred objects, your journal, etc. When you find a moment alone pull out your oasis-to-go and set it up anywhere that you feel comfortable. Voila!

creating an altar

An altar is traditionally a sacred place where ceremony and ritual are performed, found in many churches, temples, and other places of worship. In this day and age they are increasingly common in homes and even businesses. Creating an altar is a way to honor your divine self, to honor nature, love, the Universal Presence, and all things.

A QUICK LIST OF CRYSTALS AND PROPERTIES

▶ Amethyst (purple) - balances mental, emotional, and physical bodies

▶ Carnelian (red orange) - creativity, personal power, sexuality, fertility

▶ Citrine (ochre) - to increase and maintain wealth, helps perceive obstacles

▶ Garnet (wine) - for health, extracts negative energy

▶ Labradorite (metallic multi) - clears, protects, and balances the aura

▶ Peridot (green) - to cleanse, stimulate, and open the heart, inspiring happiness

▶ Rose Quartz (pink) - love, calm

▶ Tigers Eye (brown or yellow) - personal power, courage, and energy

Begin by finding the perfect location for your altar. Within your sacred space is optimal, but you can have it anywhere; on a small table, atop a dresser, or on a bookshelf. Or maybe you choose to have one in every room. You may want to locate it somewhere that will be left alone by curious hands. If you like, first place a beautiful piece of cloth on the altar. Choose some special items of meaning, a picture of yourself or a loved one, trinkets that hold a spiritual value to you. You can choose to represent the four elements on your altar. For fire use candles, or a symbol of the Sun; for Earth use a plant or rock; for air use incense or a light-blue stone or crystal; and for water, a small bowl of water or a bamboo plant securely set in a bowl of rocks and water. If you have a metaphysical store in your area, they will have lots of groovy things you can put on your altar like incense burners, little pyramids, or animal figurines. Crystals have healing properties, so you can use specific crystals to add power to your intentions by placing them on your altar.

Use your altar to acknowledge anything or any person you would like to honor. It can be used for healing yourself or others. Use it to symbolize the gratitude you have for your own life. Attend to your altar regularly, dust it and rearrange it, adding or removing items to reflect your feelings or spiritual work. Vary the theme or colors of your altar to match with the seasons, your intentions, or personal cycles. Write intentions on paper and set them on your altar under one or

THINGS TO PUT ON YOUR ALTAR:

stones ▶ special beads ▶ crystals ▶ figurines of animals or mythical creatures ▶ leaves ▶ flowers ▶ plants ▶ sea shells ▶ sea glass ▶ candles ▶ incense ▶ statues ▶ images of Buddha, or any other God symbol ▶ a sacred or special book ▶ photographs ▶ images of nature ▶ art ▶ a poem or page from your journal ▶ a slip of paper with an intention on it two of your sacred objects. Light the candles or burn the incense when you do meditations or rituals. Use it as you see fit. Enjoy.

you rock!

LOVE UP ON YOURSELF . . .

▶ Say "I love you" to yourself.

▶ Contemplate the miracle of your existence, the miracle of your body temple, the miracle of the breath of life.

▶ Go for a walk or a run, or go throw some hoops.

▶ Embrace your innocence.

▶ Stretch.

▶ Do yoga.

▶ Sing and dance wildly when no one is home.

▶ Take extravagant bubble baths with candles and wine. (men too!)

▶ Cry if you want to.

▶ Get a massage.

▶ Drum or play an instrument.

▶ Make art.

▶ Laugh for no reason, or for every reason.

▶ Go to a movie alone.

▶ Dress up and take yourself to dinner.

Do you know how magnificent you are? Really, do you? Do you at least have a healthy appreciation for yourself? How can you expect other people to enjoy your company if you don't even want to be around yourself? In a society where our attention is externally focused, it is essential to turn that focus back onto yourself.

One thing we have learned very early in life is that no one is perfect, and therein lies the problem. If no one is perfect, then we all must be messed up in one way or another. What exactly is perfection, anyway? Who or what sets the standard for perfect? What is a flaw? These perceptions vary from person to person. If being perfect means living up to our own or another's standards, then the idea of perfection is just a conditional, arbitrary form of control justifying the role of the internal judge's existence.

Most of us think there is something wrong with who we are on some level. Instead of berating ourselves for supposed imperfections and always striving for misguided, impossible standards of perfection, what if we all believed that we are perfect just the way we are? We are on our life journey to have experiences that enhance our understanding of ourselves, each other, the world, and beyond. Things we consider mistakes are usually our greatest teachers.

Who we are now is a result of all that we have been through thus far, and we still think we are not good enough. Says who? Says you, as you desperately work your hardest to convince yourself of your unworthiness. You are blinded by your own glory. There is nothing wrong with you. There is nothing to fix. Yes, there may be a few things about you that could use some healing love and attention. But you are already whole. You can't become more whole; you can only become more and more aware of the wholeness that exists within and through you. If you keep trying to fix yourself, you are only reaffirming that there is something wrong with you. Healing is different; we are here to heal the illusion of a fractured consciousness. The fractured view of reality is but a dream; our unlimited self is the true reality. True reality is free from the ropes of limitation that have bound us for so long.

How do we gain this understanding of ourselves? Through love and acceptance of ourselves. Through an awareness of ourselves as whole beings, living and loving in the cosmic soup of the Universal Presence. We begin by acknowledging ourselves as the suns, moons, and stars, the sons and daughters of the universe.

Every day, acknowledge your divine, powerful self in some way. Find new ways to give to yourself. In order to receive the full benefits of giving to yourself, you must also be ready to accept and receive from yourself.

> **"Marry yourself first, promise to never leave you."**
> **—SARK**

If you find that you are having a hard time giving to or receiving from yourself, take some time to consider why. Does it seem wrong? Is there guilt involved somehow? Do you have children or a partner, who get all your giving, till there is none left for you? Reflect on the root cause of your inability to give to yourself, or to love yourself. There are likely shadows at work that are yet to be embraced, disowned parts of you that feel unworthy of love.

When we see that our inner needs are nurtured and cared for, we will find ourselves more available to others in our lives. How can we give fully to our children and loved ones if we cannot give fully to ourselves? And what do we have to give them if we are not full of love to begin with? Feeding our souls benefits all humankind, for the vibrations flowing from you travel infinitely affecting All That Is. If you want to do something to change the world, do something to love yourself, for this love of self will ripple out into eternity. When you truly love yourself you can't help but love the World, because you can see and feel that the world is part of you, is within you.

So proclaim your wonder, accept your brilliance, quit trying to resist how extremely magnificent you are. There is humbleness in your magnificence, because you know that everyone's true self is also magnificent. And whether they know it or not, you do. You know it about you and about them.

And, don't worry, you may forget sometimes—we all do—but forgetting doesn't change the fact that you still rock!

> "Every one of us can at any moment begin to cultivate the habit of taking care of ourselves. I believe this is just a habit like any other. It is not a great mystery. And it can start in a thousand different ways. It can be a highly individual path. And it can be highly addictive in a positive sense. And the more we do it the stronger the habit becomes and the better we get at it and the more this spills over into everything we do until slowly we find ourselves becoming truly healthier and happier in every way."
>
> —JINJEE

WARRIOR WORKSHEET

Make a list of all the things that make you magnificent. Do not be modest—this is not the time or place for modesty. Claim your divinity; no one can do it for you. This worksheet is double-sided, so you can tear or cut it out and place it somewhere you can see it every day. Recite the list out loud every day until it no longer feels funny or embarrassing. As you discover more magnificence, use the other side.

I AM MAGNIFICENT!

I AM MAGNIFICENT!

URBAN SOUL WARRIOR

rise and shine

The first five to ten minutes of your morning can be the most productive part of your whole day if you use them wisely. The first few moments of your awakening are very powerful. You are reentering what you consider to be your true reality from the magical dream state.

Are you one of the millions that normally awaken to a blaring alarm clock that rudely jolts you from the bliss of rest and rejuvenation? Do you spring up joyfully from your bed, or do you curse the day? Often, as soon as we have pulled our consciousness from the state of sleep, we immediately start thinking of all the things we have to do that day, and grumpy attitudes are not an unusual occurrence. We begin by worrying about the things that we worry about, and getting our self all riled about whatever riles us up (remember how mad or disappointed we are at people we know?). We make sure we remember to feel guilty about whatever it is we feel guilty about. Then we move right into stressing about work or money or whatever gives you that early morning dose of stress. We may start our day feeling victimized by our government, our peers, bad people, or the system at large. And with that we go on about our day. We then wonder why our day, our lives, or our world seem so screwed up. Well, what do you expect? The first thoughts you have in the morning set the tempo for the whole day, day after day.

● ●

What we don't realize is that those first few thoughts are the plan of action that we subconsciously follow. Morning time is magical; it is a time of transformation, where night becomes day. We would do well to use it to our advantage. Those first ten minutes of thought can make or break your day. There are those of you, of course, who are an exception to the rule, a.k.a. the early birds who wake up all perky and ready for the world. Can it get even better, even for you? Yes.

What if you used those first precious moments to affirm what a fantastic day you are going to have, or to say or set intentions for things you would like to bring into your life? What if every morning you thought about the things in your life that you are grateful for, or the amazing people you are blessed to know? What if in the morning your first conscious thoughts were prayers or an outflow of love to others and the world?

It seems like such a simple thing, yet the effects are profound. In those first juicy moments of your morning, instead of ticking off the laundry list of things to do, decide how your day is going to go. Decide that it will be productive and will flow smoothly. Try it! Make a decision that tomorrow morning, before you even get out of bed, you are going to use those first five to ten minutes as the most productive minutes of the day. One thing that may help is getting an alarm clock that wakes you up to music or another inoffensive sound. Wouldn't you rather be awakened with a kiss than a slap? Most alarm clocks are equipped with snooze buttons. Set your clock ten minutes earlier than usual. When the alarm goes off in the morning hit the snooze button, and use those valuable minutes to create and transform your day and life. If you wake up naturally, make a commitment to not get out of bed until you have said some beautiful and positive things about yourself, your day, and your life. Do not feel pressured to fill the whole ten minutes; that is not the point. A few statements, intentions, affirmations, words of prayer, or words of gratitude will do the trick. You may even be surprised to find yourself beginning to look forward to these precious morning minutes. Maybe waking up early every morning doesn't have to suck.

Write down a few thoughts that you'd like to start your day with. The temple-building exercise on pg. 115 is a great way to begin a day, as are gratitudes on pg. 106.

heal thy emotional self!

You are in charge of healing your consciousness. Healing is a process of remembering your wholeness. Self-forgiveness is an integral part of the healing process, but there may be other things that need to heal: the emptiness caused by the death of a loved one, abuse of some kind, the break-up of a relationship, some type of addiction. Whatever it is you are dealing with, however hurtful it feels when you think about it, and no matter how much you may push it away, everything has the ability to be healed within you if you give it the opportunity. Of course, it's very common that we have difficulty releasing these painful feelings. The ego identifies heartily with suffering. People have identified so much with emotional and physical suffering, they don't know who they would be if they were no longer suffering.

Meditation is a wonderful way to introduce healing to yourself. Movement and dance also have a tremendous healing ability. Writing and journaling are great ways to bring healing energy to the things that need attention. The places that need healing are wounds, emotional wounds. These wounds are felt when someone bumps up against them, purposefully or not. When you come to understand that you have an emotional wound, cradle this part of you. Be patient and loving to this wound, it is only in need of your love and attention to heal.

}

wile out, *verb:*
to act crazy,
to act wild, to
shake and
seize the body

Using the foundation meditation in Chapter Two, meditate about the situation that brought on the wound. Feel the emotion associated with this memory, and then release it down the cord. If there is any forgiveness of self or others required to complete this process, do so. Or consider what needs to be healed and when alone put on some music and close the shades so you can *wile out* unconcerned with prying eyes or ears. Move your body, imagining you are tearing and pulling these painful memories out of your energy body and throwing them from you, stomping free of them, and filling up with sunlight.

You can write about these things as if they didn't happen to you, as if you are writing about another person, like you are telling a story. Or write in the first person. Maybe write a letter, addressing yourself or whomever else the situation might concern, describing the sadness, anger, or other feelings. Use your writing to explore how you'd like to see the situation resolve.

Have gratitude for the experience. Reflect about what you have learned and experienced from this situation that has strengthened you or given you a deeper insight. There are positive aspects to all of this even if you can't see them right now; try to envision what they are.

*   *   *

WARRIOR WORKSHEET

Are there any emotional wounds within you that need to be healed? Take a few moments to run a timeline of your life through your mind, and fill in the worksheet below.

Emotional wounds in childhood . . .

Emotional wounds in adolescence . . .

Emotional wounds in adulthood . . .

Take each of these wounds, and as hard as it is, reflect on it. Does it bring up any emotion? If it does, allow yourself to feel this pain without judging yourself or others. When you have become present to the emotion associated with this memory or wound say "peace" to it and release it.

Write about resolving these issues even if they do not yet feel completely resolved. Write about what it felt like to have the wound and what it felt like once you were able to release the wound. If you are not yet able to let it go, write about what it would feel like if you did.

molting

Have you ever found yourself in a funk that has lasted more than a day or two? Our transformation often entails giving attention to things that we didn't realize needed it. We go through cycles of birth and death regularly in our everyday lives, even if we are not aware of them. When you notice that you have been down or glum and these feelings are lasting for more than a few hours, take heart. Something wonderful is happening. Often as we grow, we begin to shed old ways of being or beliefs that no longer serve the powerful being we are becoming. What you are feeling is something that is coming up into your awareness to be released. This is the death part of the process.

Molting, *verb:* to shed periodically an outer covering such as the skin to allow for growth.

When we are conscious of this process and are gentle with ourselves, we can observe our feelings and assist in the process by allowing whatever it is we are feeling to express itself. We can monitor our feelings and become aware of what it is we are releasing by paying attention to our thought process. Sometimes an understanding of what is being released may elude you. This is fine, too. Acknowledge the process is a death cycle, or a cycle of change, molting, shedding, release—whatever you may prefer to call it.

Rejoice, for the time of birth comes next in this cycle. This difficult period is happening to make room for rebirth! Something wonderful is being born in you, a deeper connection with the universe is the end result. You are the caterpillar becoming the butterfly. For example, you may find leaving your job necessary and painful, but a great and fulfilling new career is around the corner. Or maybe you are feeling insecure in yourself or your relationship. If you allow yourself to accept the feelings you are experiencing by honoring them and releasing them they will bring a great gift—love!

One way to honor this death and birth cycle is to purchase or make a piece of jewelry, a ring, necklace, or bracelet that you wear as a symbol whenever are going through a molting process. Throughout your day as you notice this symbol, remember to be gentle with yourself, and to honor whatever feelings are asking to be released. Let go of feelings by using the foundation meditation in Chapter Two or by whatever process comes naturally to you. Send your confusion, stress, anger, or sadness out to be recycled by the Earth.

A quick release can be done at work, at a meeting, or anywhere without going into full meditation. Take two or three deep breaths and imagine you are sending these unwanted energies down into the Earth to be reprocessed. When doing this release process be sure to fill yourself with the divine light of Sun or Earth energy, as you don't want the same type of energy that was released to return.

Reflecting on your past and bringing to mind times of sadness, depression, or intense emotion that lasted for a significant period can help you recognize the next time you are going through a molting, shedding old skins to make way for the new.

WARRIOR WORKSHEET

Reflect on when you have experienced what seemed to be a longer-than-usual emotional downturn, whether sadness, anger, stagnation, unworthiness, or other low-energy emotional changes. See if you can remember the result of these experiences. How did they turn out? Did everything end up being okay? Did something come to an end, such as a relationship or job? Do you feel better off from the experience?

rebirth meditation

Doing a rebirth meditation when you are going through a molting or death process can bring you some inner peace and hasten whatever changes or growing pains you are going through. This meditation will take some time and attention, and should be done in the sanctity of your home or somewhere you will not be interrupted.

LIE DOWN IN the fetal position on the bed or on the floor using a pillow for your head if you like. You want to be comfortable and warm. Put a blanket on top of you, even covering your head if this is not uncomfortable for you. (Ignore the blanket if the weather is warm.) Begin by taking several deep breaths until you are relaxed.

Imagine yourself as an embryo in your mother's womb. Feel the weightlessness and purity of being. Feel the unconditional love that your mother (or the universe or Source) has for you. Receive that love. It is peaceful and wonderful here. Effortlessly receive the nutrients your body will use to grow. Visualize yourself growing into a fetus, being loved unconditionally and loving unconditionally.

At any time during this growth process you may decide to embody characteristics you would like to cultivate in your life (patience, kindness, generosity, etc.). As you grow you begin to feel the walls of the uterus press softly against your skin. You are being cradled in the arms of the universe. Surrender to this feeling of safety and love. At some point, when you are ready, you begin to feel the jolts of the contractions that have begun. Feel yourself being pulled toward the light of love and total acceptance as you move through the birth canal. Enter the world joyfully, for you have been reborn!

Take your time acclimating and coming out of this meditation. Stretch you arms, legs, and body. Give thanks and rejoice, you are born!

Write about your rebirth experience. Did it bring up any specific emotions or thoughts?

---

love letters

A beautiful way to nurture and support yourself is to write yourself a love letter. It is a great exercise and can be challenging. This letter should say all the wonderful things you would love to hear from those you hold dear, and the things you love about yourself or would like to love about yourself. It can contain compliments on attributes you would like to embody even if you feel you don't really represent them right now.

The point is not to write the letter from the perspective of a real person (this is not about anyone else), but to use other perspectives as a tool to detach yourself somewhat. This can give you another viewpoint so you feel freer to compliment yourself than you would otherwise. You can write from the perspective of a fictional, loving parent, as though you are the son or daughter, or from the perspective of a lover, friend, secret admirer, or mentor. You can address your letters "Dear (your name)," "My Dearest Love," or "Dear Mr. Magnificent," and so on. Of course you can always decide to write the letter from your own perspective, or first person, addressed to yourself.

● ●

Write about accomplishing your dreams, or promise to support and accept yourself through the good and the bad. Compliment yourself on a job well done, whether you have really accomplished a task or you just desire to accomplish something. Do not be afraid to admire your power and beauty, even if part of you doesn't fully believe all the words. Write about the strengths and traits you want to have as if they are already yours. It can be poetic, or not. The point is to only write in a tone of love and acceptance.

You can also integrate shadow aspects, incorporating a love for yourself as a whole is great. *For example:* I am pleased with the way you (or I, depending on the perspective) have been dealing with your anger. You have found a way to honor your whole self.

If you feel funny or embarrassed about the exercise, or are concerned with someone finding this very personal letter to yourself, when you have completed the letter put it in a private place or, if you prefer, tear it up. You may want to keep it in an old box full of memories, letters, and pictures. You can return to it over time and remind yourself of those qualities you've continued to embody or have since developed even more.

If you enjoy this exercise, do it often. Write yourself an e-mail while at the office when you have a few spare minutes. Pull out a sheet of paper and write some loving or supportive words to yourself on the subway. *Warning:* fellow passengers may wonder what that little smile is all about.

Use the following page for the letter, or write it wherever you feel comfortable.

LOVE LETTER

the art of surrender

Warriors, we who understand our connection to all life and the Source have a secret weapon others may not know about: sweet surrender. In times of confusion or stress has someone ever said to you, "just surrender to the universe"? It is powerful advice.

Usually we only think of surrender in a negative light, as giving up on something we should fight for. Here it means to let go and place your decisions and concerns in the hands of your inner guidance or higher power. Paradoxically, you will find that giving up to the infinite organizing power of the universe is an act of courage and acceptance that opens up greater possibility in your life.

> **"The Power of Surrender: Just as the miracle of nature effortlessly produces the beauty of its surroundings, you have been provided with and hold the power to effortlessly attract and create your desired miracles in each and every area of your life if only you will trust, surrender and 'allow' it to be so."** **—CHUCK DANES**

The next time you are unsure of what decision to make or just plain don't know what your next move should be, surrender. If your heart is broken or you feel hurt, surrender. If you have done something you are not proud of, and you are angry or ashamed, surrender those feelings. Surrender the frustrations or stress you are feeling at the office. When you are not sure which way to go in a relationship you are involved in, surrender to love. If you can't figure out how to make something work, or you can't see the solution to a problem, surrender it. Then just leave it alone, strip the thought from your mind for as long as you can. If it returns incessantly, keep surrendering it for as long as you need to.

When you surrender you are releasing resistance and opening yourself to the flow of your inner guidance. When we resist or try too hard we are essentially paddling upstream. When you let go and trust your inner wisdom, or the wisdom of God, or the wisdom inherent in Nature you are in the flow, which allows the river of life to take you to the ideal place or situation for your highest growth and love. The power of surrender is a life-changing and vital principle in empowering yourself.

You will find the results can be amazing—when the time is right, you will intuitively know the answer, or your heart will heal, or the stress will dissipate, or the solution to your situation will be revealed. Stay open and alert for the answer or direction best suited to your needs.

Have you ever surrendered a problem, issue, feeling, or decision to the universe or God? If so, what was the result? Whether or not you have consciously surrendered something in the past, what are some things you could surrender now?

cosmic seed

Most of us city folks don't have the luxury of much nature and veg-etation in our immediate surroundings. Although parts of some cities have grass lawns, flowers, and an abundance of trees, more often grass is found only in selected parks, trees are rare, and flow-ers are only found in boxes on windowsills.

The power and peaceful effects that nature can have in our lives are not dependent upon our proximity to natural areas such as golf courses, parks, or the country and mountains. We ourselves are a part of nature, so we have only to access it with our minds and hearts to partake in its rejuvenating wonder.

● ●

How often do you contemplate the exquisite humbleness of a seed? In each tiny seed exists the potential of the whole. The entire splen-dor of the great oak is contained in one little acorn. A seed sprouts and grows into a plant or sapling, bush or tree, completely and effortlessly supported by life itself. Sun, earth, air, and water give of their very essence that life may live.

We are cosmic seeds, beings of light that have traveled endlessly through galaxies unnumbered. We are scattered across the infinite universe. Many of us having landed on this blue planet for a cycle (or many) of earthly experience. We are seeds of pure potential, our lives completely sustained by life—unless, of course, we choose resistance. Life then supports that choice and reflects our resistance back to us. We have innate access to an effortless, ever unfolding, fully supported, and nurtured life experience.

The following is inspired by Paulo Coelho's seed exercise. This is a wonderful meditation and visualization, to put you in touch with your bountiful sustenance, life.

* * *

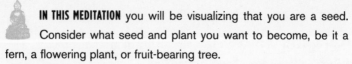

IN THIS MEDITATION you will be visualizing that you are a seed. Consider what seed and plant you want to become, be it a fern, a flowering plant, or fruit-bearing tree.

Start by getting into a comfortable position. Bring yourself to a calm and relaxed state and take several deep breaths. When you are ready, imagine you are the seed you have chosen. You don't have to know exactly what the seed looks like, just be the seed. You are surrounded by the cool, damp arms of Earth. All is dark. You begin to feel life inside of you as the moisture begins to soften your shell. Suddenly a root shoots out, reaching out into the darkness to suck more of the sweet, delicious wetness from the musky Earth. You soon become aware of a sprout uncurling from your center, pushing upward against the soft forgiving soil, longing for the warmth radiating from above. This warmth is beckoning you. You continue to grow, lengthening, extending, the Earth making way for your journey. With a little push you break through the topsoil and are greeted by the glaring sun and the rush of the wind, both of who are rejoicing at your arrival. You feel your cells instinctively absorbing the air and extracting nutrients from it. Clouds gather to witness, and, soon a gentle rain too, is celebrating the miracle of you. You stretch and grow, leaves unfurling endlessly, it seems. Part of you is safe and deep in the cool Earth, the rest of you basking in the glory of the Sun, Moon, and Stars. Move through the cycle of budding and the delight of flowering, and then bearing fruit (if your plant does these things). Enjoy your plant self for as long as you please. When you are ready, give thanks for the experience, and open your eyes.

You can stand and stretch your arms as you grow through this exercise if that feels natural. This exercise can be used when you feel in need of a new start. It is also good for healing, as plants have many healing properties. Select a plant that has healing properties specific to your particular ailment. Do this meditation often (once a week), changing your plant, or use the same plant over and over to get the concentrated healing effects of your chosen plant.

Write about your experience. What plant did you choose? How did it feel to embody this form of life?

an attitude of gratitude

The power of gratitude is beyond measure. It is by the grace of gratitude that we can come through traumatic and turbulent times unscathed, stronger and ready for the world. Gratitude is often overlooked. Even those who are thankful of the good things in their lives are likely using only a small percentage of its potential.

> "Gratitude unlocks the fullness of life. It turns what we have into enough, and more. It turns denial into acceptance, chaos to order, confusion to clarity. It can turn a meal into a feast, a house into a home, a stranger into a friend. Gratitude makes sense of our past, brings peace for today, and creates a vision for tomorrow." **—MELODY BEATTIE**

Gratitude is a message to the universe that your arms are open to receive. The universe takes that message and reflects back to you more to be grateful for. It is that easy. When you are grateful you naturally magnetize more of what it is you are grateful for. To receive, you must be thankful for all you already have.

As simple as it seems, gratitude may be one of the most overlooked and undervalued expressions. Many give thanks for their food before each meal. And many say thank you daily out of politeness. But how often are we thankful for the miracle of the human form we are so blessed to inhabit? How often do we think about the people in our lives that have cared for us, loved us, and profoundly affected who we are? Are you regularly grateful to have a roof over your head? Are you grateful for the clothes on your back, no matter how raggedy or second-handish some of them may be?

It does not stop there. Be grateful for each breath that allows this body life. Be grateful that the sun shines, that the wind blows. Be grateful that you have water running through pipes in your home that allow you to flush the stench of your waste away, to wash from you the stress of the day. Once you take time to consider all that we have, rich or poor, you will be amazed at the ongoing list you can come up with: the laugh of your child, the kiss of your lover, the smell of your mami's cooking. When you begin to take notice, even the most trivial things take on wonder.

Cultivating an attitude of gratitude will have a profound effect on even the most mundane, dramatic, and otherwise unenjoyable moments of our lives. Every event, especially and including the ones that bring us heartache and pain, has a gift, a seed with the potential to grow something phenomenal in us: awareness. When you are suffering, whether from a broken heart or a broken arm, if you can find it in yourself to have gratitude, you will find your term of suffering shortened. The pain is lessened. You have decided to search for the jewel, and the jewel you shall find.

How can I be grateful in times of loss and pain, you ask? It is during this time that reasons for gratitude may surely elude you. Fear not. You may say, *I am grateful, for I know there is a gift of growth and love somewhere within this pain.* Make an effort to explore any positive effects from the experience. Or, if after much thought you still cannot see how you might benefit in some way from a difficult experience, be grateful for the things you know you are grateful for. The good thing is that, with gratitude, now you can create the coming moments with love and awareness.

• •

Just find the gratitude. Let it surround you and follow you around. As the moments pass, relief will come in some form or another. The gratitude may do nothing but help you get through the moment. Acceptance is also a form of gratitude. If you can't seem to find the feeling of gratitude in your experience, acceptance will go a long way in its stead. With acceptance, you acknowledge you can't change *what is* right at this moment, so you release the resistance. Remember, what you resist persists, which makes it harder to see the lessons of your situation. If you can begin with acceptance, you are well on your way to gratitude.

When gratitude becomes a real part of your life you will understand what all this fuss is about. Gratitude is not something that can be explained so well in words, for it is a feeling, a fullness that wells within you. As it becomes part of you, you will find yourself effortlessly having bursts of gratitude throughout the day. Gratitude is a great thing to start your day with. Add it to your *rise and shine* ritual from pg. 89.

We should express gratitude not only for the things we already have in our lives, but for the things that are coming into our lives. Be grateful that your true love, or your new home, or financial prosperity is coming into your life. Whatever it is, be grateful now. What are you waiting for? If you can't be grateful now, that only shows that you don't really believe you are going to get to experience your heart's desires. Be grateful for all the joy, love, and abundance you have now, and all that is on its way to you!

WARRIOR WORKSHEET

Write a list of five to ten things that you are sincerely grateful for. Write today's date on it and also the date thirty days from now. The worksheet is double-sided, so tear it out of this book and post it somewhere will you will see it every day, like on the bathroom mirror or refrigerator. If you don't want to post it, make a commitment to yourself to look at the list every day. Read it out loud every day, and do it with feeling—you must feel the gratitude; you are not a robot. Do this list for at least thirty days. You may want to add to it as you go along. When you reach the thirtieth day, flip the list and start a new one. You are now on the road to cultivating an attitude of gratitude.

*   *   *

I AM GRATEFUL . . .

I AM GRATEFUL . . .

chillin' with the ancestors . . .

We all have ancestors, and we can't escape 'em. They are all around us. They are in us, we are representing them. Their DNA makes up our very being. They are likely chillin' with us right now, like it or not. Not in the form of ghosty spirits haunting around, but in the form of loving, wise energy that we can tap into.

Your ancestors are willing to offer you guidance and wisdom in your life path. They are your powerful, ethereal support system. This guidance comes in the form of messages in your daily life, things you may consider coincidences or symbols that have a special meaning for you. You may intuitively discover some karma that needs to be healed in your family line by honoring your ancestors.

You can still connect with the loving energy of your ancestors even if you don't know your family history. The energy of your family line from the beginning of time is within you, within each vein and cell. The following is a meditation that can open up your connection with them.

honoring your ancestors

SIT OR STAND in a comfortable position and prepare as you would for any meditation. Observe your breath for a time, and when you are ready, call to your ancestors. For example, "Dear loving ancestors, spirits of those from whom I descend, I honor you. I am you." When calling to them, make some mention of love; this way you will only attract those who work in love and light. Be still for a few moments and imagine that your ancestors are sitting around you in a circle. Be at peace with this energy. You may see actual faces, or maybe just shadowy forms in your mind's eye. You may not see anything but may feel it. And if you don't see or feel it, don't worry, they have heard your call and are with you, and they can hear you. Ask them for their guidance and wisdom, thank them for the gifts they have brought to you. Request that they walk with you and protect you. You may light a candle, incense, or sage as an offering to them. When you feel the meditation is complete, offer them thanks for their presence. Open your eyes.

Write about your experience.

MIND YOUR
TEMPLE

CITY LIFE can be hard on the body and its systems. We breathe toxic fumes that are made by all the things we think we cannot live without—cars, products, technology. Many of us eat foods made with chemicals that have names we cannot even pronounce, or things that are deep-fried to an unrecognizable crisp. We go to bed too late and are up too early. If we walk a lot, our bodies are constantly absorbing the shock of the cement underfoot. If we spend a lot of time commuting then we likely don't get the exercise essential to a healthy body. If you are a city dweller and in good health, congratulations! If not, join the club—the health club. Just kidding! It is not a bad idea, of course, but a healthy body is a reflection of a healthy, balanced mind, with a healthy understanding or connection with its divine self. A healthy body means healthy through and through. You can be a hottie on the outside and in desperate need of health on the inside.

It is not unusual for people to be detached from their bodies, to not be aware of what is going on within them or be attuned to the sensations of the body. Our bodies are alive and conscious. Each system is conscious, each organ is conscious, and each and every cell is conscious. The body is your temple. Some people consider church the temple of God and will go their whole lives denying that God is within them. The body is a sacred place. It knows what it is doing at every second. If it seems like it is out of whack, it is trying to tell you that some part of your mental self is out of whack or that your connection to your spiritual self is out of whack.

Is it true that people can just think themselves healthier? In general people don't believe that they can affect their own health merely by having a positive thought process. Your physical being and condition are a reflection of whatever you believe about yourself. Some try for awhile, but give up if they don't see instant results. But it is not just positive thoughts that can create health and balance in the body, it is also the connection with our deepest self, which aligns the body with wholeness. Healing and rejuvenating the self takes attention and some discipline. The light of attention on your body is like the sun on flowers. What you shine your light on grows and blossoms. Each body, like each life, holds lessons for growth and understanding.

The body, each and every body, is a magnificent creation. It takes its sustenance from the environment, extracts useful nutrients, and rids itself of what if cannot use. Every organ in a healthy body works in sync with every other organ. The blood carries oxygen and nutrition to every single cell. The immune system is constantly at work to keep balance within the whole system. And this all happens automatically without our direct attention, and often without our appreciation.

And the mind, that is a whole topic to itself. It is the center of all activity; it is the tool by which all automatic function operates. It interprets the information we receive from the five amazing senses that allow us to experience ourselves and our environment. Not only does the mind operate our magnificent body, it thinks too, and is also aware that it is thinking. The mind can be our greatest tool or the reason for our demise. The state of the world today is a product of our mind, personally and collectively. The state of our physical and mental health is a product of the mind. When you have a healthy mind you will live both in a healthy body and a healthy reality.

It is not difficult to bridge that disconnection with our bodies.

All it takes is attention; mindfulness. Mindfulness may take practice at first, mostly because of our detachment from the body, but then it becomes a glorious practice. When you begin to give attention and love to the body, it rejoices and returns the love. You will feel more amazing and beautiful; you will have more energy, and excitement for life. You will fall in love with yourself like never before, because you are *alive* and you know it, you can feel it.

temple-building

> "The moment I have realized God sitting in the temple of every human body, the moment I stand in reverence before every human being and see God in him – that moment I am free from bondage, everything that binds vanishes, and I am free."
>
> **—SWAMI VIVEKANANDA**

The temple of our body is an amazing place. It is truly miraculous. It performs millions of daily functions, most of which the average Joe knows nothing about. It is compromised of systems that perform in sync with each other to carry out the daily functions of digestion, elimination, circulation, and many, many more. The body is not separate from the mind; it is privy and reactive to all your thoughts and actions. The body is conscious, too. Not just as a whole, but every system, every organ, every cell is conscious, every cell has a soul.

Most of us have lost touch with our bodies. We are familiar, even obsessed, with the way they look on the outside, but we don't pay much attention to what they feel like inside, or even what it feels like to be alive. It is often this disconnection with our temple that causes many of our illnesses. Stop for a moment and close your eyes, and feel the life in your body. You are alive. Your organs are alive. Every cell is living and breathing, experiencing what you are experiencing.

An amazing way to start the day, as well as to program your subconscious to manifest a healthy body, is to build your body fresh every day. This exercise is about creating your temple in the best, most healthy and beautiful image you can imagine. If at first the exercise seems tedious, this is where discipline comes in. Retraining the mind and body for health and longevity takes focus and attention. This is an exercise that you could do every day for the rest of your life. This process honors each part of you as a living breathing entity, empowering every aspect of your physical being with love.

● ◗

EVERY MORNING, EVEN before you get out of bed (if it is realistic for you), begin by bringing attention to your body, starting whereever makes most sense to you. This could be the head, or the toes, or maybe you want to begin from the inside out, and you begin with the skeletal system. Imagine your bones are strong and healthy, and thank them for being so. Thank every organ for functioning in conjunction with every other organ. Think about your muscles and imagine them strong and healthy. See your skin as smooth and vibrant, see your muscles taut and toned. Talk to your organs and systems, tell them how much you appreciate the wonderful job they are doing for you. Run your tongue over your teeth one by one and over every surface of your mouth, loving it. If you have requests, gently ask your body parts to align themselves with your desires. If you have any particular issues in the body, give those places special attention, visualizing those areas in full health, and fully functioning. See yourself, the whole of you, as strong, healthy, beautiful, and unaffected by time and changing environmental factors. Attend to your amazing miracle of a body and watch it become more magnificent under your shining attention.

shake that thang!

Warriors, so powerful are we in soul, mind, and body. The amazing temple that you are so blessed to inhabit takes maintenance. In order for it to work smoothly we must keep it well fed, lubricate it with water, and make sure to keep it moving.

The body can do some cool moves. It has amazing natural strength and endurance that can be built up to even greater levels. It has great flexibility, and rhythm. Technology has created such convenience in our world that many of our bodies rarely experience the joys of movement. Some of us have long commutes by car or bus every day, or get so accustomed to driving everywhere that we get out of the habit of walking as part of our daily routine.

This type of lifestyle invites atrophy into your body quite early. The body begins to waste away, to stop working properly due to poor nourishment and lack of exercise. There are other causes of atrophy, such as poor circulation and disease. When there is little or no movement, toxins build up in the bodily organs, bones, and tissues. These toxins may come from things like pesticides in foods, or they may be emotional toxins from repressed feelings or experiences.

The body was created to move. Movement raises the heart rate, which gets the blood pumping. Physical activity oxygenates the blood and increases the rate of metabolism. The body wakes up, feels alive, and creates even more energy. You feel happier and more complete.

Moving your body doesn't mean you have to run laps around the park. Running regularly takes endurance and discipline, and is an excellent way to exercise the body, but it is not realistic for everybody. Yoga is a wonderful practice of mindfulness and stretching that you may find more your speed. Stretching the body slowly, bringing your full attention to the part of the body that is being stretched, works wonders. There are many ways to practice yoga. You can take a class, or buy a book or video and do exercise in the privacy of your own home.

Dancing is a great way to move. Going out to the club is a great way to exercise, if you can avoid the heavy drinking scene. You can dance at home, close the blinds, and lock the doors so you won't be disturbed. Put on some of your favorite music as loud as you can stand it, and go for it. If you live with other people, or in an apartment with thin walls, put on headphones to jam. It doesn't matter what you look like, there is no one watching. Shake and shiver and jump and slide. Wake your body up from your head to the tips of your toes. If you feel your inhibitions making themselves known, blindfold yourself. Wile out!

No matter what sort of activity you do, practicing mindfulness as you do it allows you to really tune into the body and appreciate its movements. You will feel more grounded and present, more efficient in how you move, and be less likely to injure yourself. Get into the habit of feeling the life in your body by placing your attention there, it will tell you exactly what it needs.

for the love of food

You are what you eat. We have all heard that one before. It is a literally true statement. Not only does the body break down and absorb the physical food, it absorbs the energetic nature of the food. Eating is one of the most enjoyable activities we humans do, or at least it can be. The joy of eating has been tainted by many issues—guilt, unhealthy ingredients, and processing are just the tip of the iceberg.

Soul Warriors, it is a great idea to take some time to reflect upon your relationship with food. Do you enjoy your food? Do you feel like you eat well? Overeat? Do you eat fresh or whole foods, like fruits and vegetables? Or foods made from scratch containing few or no processed ingredients? We eat so many heavily processed foods without thinking about what they contain—cheese puffs, chicken nuggets, white bread, and so on.

It is very important, as you are becoming aware of your true self, that you also become conscious of what you are putting into your precious temple. When your body is in alignment with good health you will have more room for joy.

People tend to eat what is on their plate without considering the life lived by the plant or animal before it arrived at the store. Whatever the animal or plant experienced in its life prior to you ingesting it, you then absorb. This means if animals are treated cruelly and inhumanely and live miserable lives, you then unconsciously take on this energy just by having bacon and eggs in the morning. Not to mention the growth hormones you inadvertently consume. Pesticides on fruits and vegetables cause harm most directly to the Earth and to workers who farm the land, not to mention consumers. These fruits and vegetables are not only toxic from the chemicals sprayed on them, but are emotionally toxic as well. We are what we eat, as individuals and as a society.

Buying organic fruits, vegetables, meats, and dairy products is the best way to go. There is less suffering involved in organic farming practices. Certified organic companies have to meet strict standards, and do not use synthetic pesticides. Animals raised for organic meat are not treated with hormones and other chemicals. Organic food often costs more than its counterpart, but aren't you worth it. If you aren't, who is? The truth is, the more people who buy organic, the cheaper it becomes because the demand increases. Even if you're on a tight budget, be aware that not all organic produce is super expensive. One of the best ways to buy organic is through farmer's markets, which set up in most cities across the nation at least once a week. Not only will you find cheaper produce than in the stores, but you are supporting family-run and other independent farms. Most cities also have community gardens, so you could even get to participate in nurturing an inner-city garden and cultivate relationships with your neighbors along the way. If you can't afford to buy entirely organic food right now, you can still make decisions around the most important foods to buy organic—

foods that have a soft and highly absorbent skin and soak up more of the chemicals sprayed on them. Some examples include straw-berries (or any berry), pears, tomatoes, lettuce, or any leafy greens. Fruits with a thick skin, such as oranges, avocados, and bananas, are safer. You can find more detailed listings of the safety levels of pesticide-sprayed foods online.

No matter where your food comes from, take the time to honor it. Express gratitude for the nutrients it will provide you. If it is meat, honor the life of the animal that has given its life so that you may partake of its energy. Give thanks to the farmers who have grown and harvested this food that you may have it at your table. A few simple words, while preparing and before consumption can make an amazing difference in your overall health.

What is your current relationship with food?

body of light

The aura is your energy or light body. Your physical body is the smallest and most dense part of your energy body, your physical self is extra concentrated light energy. A healthy aura extends three feet in all directions. This means (especially if you live in the city) we are all walking around in each other's light bodies! As we move through our day, the energy in our light bodies affects and is affected by all the other auras it has been near or passed through. The light body carries in it memories and remnants of emotional experiences. This is why it is a great idea to cleanse it occasionally. Your physical body naturally excretes unneeded waste every day. How often do we take a moment to consciously release the energetic waste we acquire through our day?

aura cleanse

BEGIN BY SITTING or standing in a comfortable position. Breathe deeply for a few moments until you feel relaxed. Concentrate fully on the breath and visualize with each exhale that you are pushing your aura out to its full three-foot radius from your physical self. This means three feet from the top of your head, three feet into the Earth, three feet in front of you and behind you. Pay special attention to the back area as this is often where the aura is short of its three-foot extension. Breathe your aura to its full extension for a few minutes. Some of you may experience a feeling that the aura is actually extended more than three feet. This is not unusual and results in a person being overextended and tired. With each inhale, breathe your aura in until it feels like you have contained it within three feet of your body.

Visualize a green cord at the base of your spine (a root works too) that reaches deep into the Earth. Feel the comfort as the earth supports your work. Now, choosing a method that works for you, imagine that you are cleaning any unwanted stress or funky energy out of your aura. Some suggestions: Imagine the cord is a vacuum and is sucking the funk out; or imagine the unwanted energy is gray and is released with each exhale; or visualize a funnel cloud swirling around you, sweeping all of the useless energy down into the cord. Play around with any ideas until you find the one that works best for you. Remember that this energy will be recycled, just like the waste of a compost pile or the waste of animals is used to fertilize crops and plants.

When you feel you have sufficiently cleaned out your energy body, imagine light coming into your feet, or through the crown of your head, filling your aura with golden light. Let it fill all the places that you have emptied of negative energy.

When you are ready, give thanks and open your eyes.

chakratastic!

The chakras are an energy system by which we beings are made manifest, and through which we experience the miracle of our divine temple. The most commonly known chakras are the seven that are located on the physical body.

There are many additional chakras, some in the physical body, and some above the head and under the feet. These chakras allow for an extended awareness beyond the physical body as well as a connection with one's spirit, the earth, and the endless universe.

Here is a brief description of the seven bodily chakras. Chakra energy spirals out from the spine in two directions, both in front and behind the person.

★ The first chakra is called the ROOT CHAKRA. It is red and is located at the base of the spine. This chakra represents the connection with the earth and the material realm. It is by this chakra that we are connected with life on this planet as a whole. It is important to balance this chakra because when ruled by this chakra one is a slave to his or her desires.

★ The second is called the SACRAL CHAKRA. It is orange and located under the belly button. This chakra governs creation; this is where the miracle of human life happens. This chakra is the source of all creative energy. When feeling creative blockage, or sexual dissatisfaction, consider this chakra. This chakra is our feeling center, the seat of our emotions.

★ The third is the SOLAR PLEXUS CHAKRA. It is yellow and located under your diaphragm, or at the base of the rib cage in the front of the body. It is the power chakra and governs the will. It is your source of power, and is also where you discern the power of others.

★ The fourth is the HEART CHAKRA. It is green and is located in the center of the chest. This is where real love flows through you. When this chakra is opened, the judge that lives within is no longer in complete control of you: you are open to loving and being loved. From this place you love without condition, and you are in the flow of love.

★ The fifth is the THROAT CHAKRA. It is blue and is located at the base of the throat and governs communication, the ability to speak creatively and expressively, and the ability to speak truth.

★ The sixth, also known as the THIRD EYE, is indigo and is located in the center of the forehead. This chakra governs the intuition and higher mental processes, visualization, and inspiration.

★ The seventh is the CROWN CHAKRA. It is violet or white, and is located on the top center of the skull. It represents and facilitates a relationship with the higher self and the Universal Presence.

The care of chakras is simple: attention and love. These things will keep them balanced, with life energy flowing freely along them. When they are unbalanced and blocked you see the effects in your life. The first two chakras are the most base; they are the instinctive chakras and represent all the primal issues around survival—food, sex, fight or flight.

chakra cleanse

The chakra cleanse can have a real impact on very specific elements of your life. You may decide to cleanse one chakra per meditation, giving each one lots of energy and love. Or do a full cleanse, one after the other in succession, starting with the root, during a single meditation.

WHEN IN MEDITATION, consider the chakra you are focusing on, visualize its location in the body, and focus on its color. Imagine that any unneeded or outworn energy or blockage is released. Then fill it with white or golden light. Ask your divine self to balance and align your chakras with what is spiritually ideal for you right now, in your present moment.

ELEMENTAL
AFFINITY

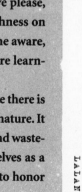

WE ARE ALL children of the Earth, and by the grace of the four elements, which sustain all life on this planet, we experience life as we know it.

earth mama

Our sweet mother Earth, she is truly a Goddess. This amazing entity has allowed us to live on and amongst her elements for several hundred thousand years. She has been patient with us as a nurturing parent is with a mischievous and troublesome child. We as a society have turned our back on her, taking as we please, without offering anything in return. But even this selfishness on our part is in alignment with our evolution. As we become aware, we remember our connection with the great Earth. We are learning again to honor her.

We city dwellers often forget how to relate to Earth since there is not much in our immediate environment to remind us of nature. It is our cities that need the most healing. The carelessness and wasteful way we treat the Earth is the same way we treat ourselves as a society. We have dishonored the Earth because we forgot to honor our true selves. We need to heal ourselves to heal the Earth.

Connecting with the Earth on a daily basis is a simple process. When you wake up in the morning, greet the Earth. When you see a bird fly by, or if you hear its song, say hello. When you walk past a tree, touch its bark with a loving hand. Decide that each step you take is a kiss from your feet to the Earth. There are many fun and wonderful ways that you can include an awareness and gratitude for the Earth in your daily life.

Embracing principles of the "green" movement is a major way to contribute to the Earth's healing. Recycle, but more importantly, limit your use of disposable containers in the first place, and reuse items whenever you can. Bring reusable bags when shopping. This is a biggie! Bike to work or school if you can. Buy organic as often as possible, including clothing and coffee as well as food. Turn the lights off, and unplug appliances when they're not in use, which will help reduce your energy bills and cut down on emissions. Turn off the water while you brush your teeth.

As you become more aware of your true self, you will naturally become more aware of your surroundings, which are but reflections of you. Offer love and attention to your Earth and you will experience even more harmony with all life.

The grounding pg. 19 and cosmic seed pg. 102 meditations are great ways to connect and honor Earth.

just breathe, baby . . .

When one really takes a moment to contemplate the great miracle of life, there is only wonder. The body is a miracle in itself, with all its automatic functions happening without our knowledge or understanding. One of the most magical things we can experience is the breath of life. Our bodies are completely connected to the atmosphere by the requirement of oxygen. No matter where you go and what you do, the whole time you are always breathing.

Consider air as the Creator, moving, flowing everywhere at once, in everyone at once. The particles you are breathing contain all life;

you are breathing the same air as everyone else on the planet, as everyone who was ever alive did. Some will say that we do not breathe the air, that the air breathes us. The interconnectedness of all things becomes apparent when one considers air and its flow and function. Oxygen is essential for cellular respiration. The millions of plant species on this beautiful Earth create the oxygen we breathe using photosynthesis. Plants create oxygen from sunlight, water, and carbon dioxide. The resulting "waste" is truly a gift, the oxygen that we breathe. The carbon dioxide released by both humans and animals when oxygen is absorbed in turn creates essential life-giving energy for plant life, and so the cycle continues.

Breathing exercises and meditations centered on the breath are good to calm and center the system. Visualize the breath as the essence of love. With each breath it gives you more life, again and again, endlessly bringing you life as you reside in your body. This is a powerful vision, as we often feel like we are lacking love. We all want to be loved, and we are. We can imagine that each breath is pure love moving through us with the gift of life, loving each and every one of our cells, promoting life. Visualize this love as the air moves in and around you, sustaining life and removing toxins from your body.

The essential meditation pg. 16 is a simple meditation that focuses on the breath.

the joy of water

Water is a miraculous element. It is so essential to our survival, yet it is terribly underappreciated by people, corporations, and governments. Our water supplies, and the great wild waters of our lakes, rivers, and oceans are under constant attack from polluters.

Dr. Masaru Emoto made some now famous discoveries about water and energy. He experimented with writing words on containers of water, and then freezing the water and examining the water crystals under a microscope. The words that were written on the water containers varied—there were positive words like love, compassion, happiness, and negative words like hate and anger. He then took pictures of the amazing results and compiled them into several books, the first of which was called *The Hidden Messages in Water*.

Dr. Emoto found that the water responded to the energy of the words they came in contact with. The crystals near life-affirming, positive words made beautiful, shimmering crystals, and the water crystals coming from containers with negative or unhappy emotions were misshapen.

This study is amazing! This means every thought and feeling we have is affecting every molecule of water within us. And this information affects us profoundly because our bodies are made up of over 70 percent water. We are what we eat, but we also are what we drink and think.

Love water! Bless water before you drink it. Bless or be grateful to every glass of water; you can transform the water by your thoughts and feelings into healing nectar for the mind and body. And drink more water! Your body will thank you. When you take a shower, thank the water, honor it. Be grateful for the water that is pouring over your body, awakening your senses, making you fresh for the world. As often as you can, use green products that do not contaminate the water supply, and use water filters to purify the tap water you drink (and realize that the source of most bottled water is the same as that tap water—so forget those plastic bottles!).

Any time you come near a body of water, be it lake or ocean, offer your gratitude for the life it brings you.

this is why I'm hot

The element of fire is so prevalent in our daily lives that we barely notice it. It is the Sun shining down on us from above, giving us life.

The Sun has been known by many cultures as God or life-giver. Early cultures were immersed in the glory of the Sun and knew it to be responsible for the life-giving foods they ate and for warmth. Without the Sun there would be no life on Earth. Plants make both food and oxygen out of sunlight, sustaining animals and people. The Sun also provides us with Vitamin D, which is a necessary nutrient in the regulation of the liver, kidneys, and bones. We absorb this nutrient directly from the Sun into our skin. Because there is so much fear of getting cancer from overexposure to the Sun, people wear sunblock so often that they also block the healthy absorption of sunlight. Wait at least ten to fifteen minutes after going outside before putting on sunblock.

Greet the Sun upon awakening, or when you go outside for the first time each day. Honor it by saying or thinking how grateful you are for the gifts brought by the Sun. Light candles during your meditations or any time to acknowledge the power of fire. There is a wonderful sequence of yoga poses you can do to honor both the Sun and your body called a *Sun Salutation*. You can find these poses in most yoga books, or by doing a search on the Internet.

standing sun pose

STAND STRAIGHT, feet parallel, and breathe out to a count of three. Inhale to a count of three as you raise your arms up and out to the side until they are overhead. Stretch and look up. Hold your breath for a count of three, then exhale to a count of three as you bend forward from the hips, keeping your head between your out-stretched arms. Try to match your breath to your movements so that you don't finish exhaling until your arms reach all the way down. Touch the floor if you can.

Exhale for a count of three as you grasp your legs firmly with both hands; bend your elbows, keeping your arms close to your sides, and pull your upper body gently toward your legs. Pull with your arms, not your stomach or back muscles. If you find it hard to grasp your ankles, hold on to your legs firmly (wherever is comfortable for you). Now release your legs and inhale to a count of three as you straighten up, keeping your arms loose at first and then out to the sides and overhead again, so that you finish your inhale when your arms are overhead. Then exhale to a count of three as you lower your arms to your sides. Relax.

SACRED
WRITING SPACE

these precious pages are here for you to be and
do what you will, enjoy . . .

doodle,
rant,
rave,
wish,
record your dreams, poetry, quotes,
love letters,
to-do list expand . . .

"Peace is not something you wish for; it's something you make, something you do, something you are, and something you give away."

—ROBERT FULGHUM,
author of *All I Need to Know I Learned in Kindergarten*

> "We have a choice: to plow new ground or let the weeds grow."
>
> —ANONYMOUS

"For attractive lips, speak words of kindness . . . For lovely eyes, seek out the good in people. For a slim figure, share your food with the hungry. For beautiful hair, let a child run his/her fingers through it once a day. For poise, walk with the knowledge that you never walk alone . . . People, even more than things, have to be restored, renewed, revived, reclaimed, and redeemed; never throw out anyone. Remember, if you ever need a helping hand, you will find one at the end of each of your arms. As you grow older, you will discover that you have two hands; one for helping yourself, and the other for helping others."

—AUDREY HEPBURN

"He who knows Self as the enjoyer of the honey from the flowers of the senses, ever present within, ruler of time, goes beyond fear. For this Self is Supreme!"

—The Upanishads, sacred Hindu scriptures

> "Self-control will place a man among the Gods, while lack of it will lead him into deepest darkness. Guard your self-control as a precious treasure, for there is no greater wealth in life than this."
>
> *—Tirukkural* 13: 121-122

"Though no one can go back and make a brand new start, anyone can start from now and make a brand new ending."

—CARL BARD, theologian

"Every man is a damn fool for at least five minutes every day; wisdom consists in not exceeding the limit."

—ELBERT HUBBARD, author, artist, and philosopher

"The foolish man seeks happiness in the distance, the wise grows it under his feet."

—JAMES OPPENHEIM, poet and author

"One cannot think crooked and walk straight."

—ANONYMOUS

"Your vision will become clear only when you look into your heart. Who looks outside, dreams. Who looks inside, awakens." —CARL JUNG, psychologist

"My life is my message."   —MAHATMA GANDHI

> "There are no accidents . . . there is only some purpose that we haven't yet understood."

> —DEEPAK CHOPRA, author and spiritual teacher

"Are you fit company for the person you wish to become?"

—ANONYMOUS

"People often say that 'beauty is in the eye of the beholder,' and I say that the most liberating thing about beauty is realizing that you are the beholder. This empowers us to find beauty in places where others have not dared to look, including inside ourselves."

—SALMA HAYEK

"Nothing will ever be attempted if all possible objections must be overcome first." —ANONYMOUS

> "I think it pisses God off if you walk by the color purple in a field somewhere and don't notice it."
>
> —ALICE WALKER, author of *The Color Purple*

ALCHEMY

AN ALCHEMIST is someone who can make amazing transformations. Tales are told of alchemists who could turn lead into gold. Alchemy has come to symbolize the evolution from ignorance to enlightenment. Soul Warriors are also alchemists; we are magically transforming our lives, beginning with our very thoughts.

We begin this transformation by becoming conscious about the thoughts, feelings, and emotions we are putting into action. In our external reality it is these thoughts, feelings (especially our feelings), and actions that attract our experiences. Whether or not you know how to use them, they are the tools used in the creation of your everyday world. Thought, though one of the subtlest forces, has tremendous powers. Even the slightest thought creates ripples through the universe. The deeper the emotion associated with a thought, the more complete the result.

There are two mental processes by which we affect our personal reality. The conscious or deciding mind makes choices all day: should you go left or right, should you eat this or that, should you go to bed now or later, do you like something or not? It makes every decision that you are living and reflecting in your world right now. Are you rich, poor, happy, in love, healthy? The deciding mind most often bases these choices on past experience, habit, religion, morals, and your conditioning. It gets its data from the external material world.

> "Subjective (subconscious) mind will never change its own nature, but will always reflect to the thinker what he thinks into it. Man did not make this law nor can he change it; but, like any other law, once understood, it becomes an obedient servant." —ERNEST HOLMES

The subconscious or creative mind carries out the orders it has received from the deciding mind. It has no bias and is unconcerned with such things as right and wrong. It does not decide whether a choice made by the objective mind is good for you or not. Its job is to make manifest the idea, image, or emotion that has been impressed upon it. The subconscious/creative mind goes to work at once to produce anything that is given to it no matter what the impending result may be. The subconscious is also a storage locker full of memories of past experiences. Here is where you store and process events, feelings, beliefs, opinions, truths, and expectations. These experiences become impressions and create grooves in the subconscious mind. With the law of inertia at work it is natural for your habitual responses to be your default point of reference, giving birth to tendencies. But do not fear, your creative, subconscious mind has an all-access pass to the infinite universe; it is swimming in it. It has eternal contact with pure potential.

With focus and attention we can change our thought patterns to recognize our magnificent potential. Our subconscious/creative mind will then effortlessly attract the appropriate circumstances from limitless possibilities to reflect this greater understanding.

These are the instruments by which we develop our extraordinary lives. Thought energy has the power of creation around it at all times. A thought becomes immensely stronger if an emotional feeling is associated with it. Emotion makes a mere thought into an actual sensation that you experience in your physical self. When an emotion is impressed upon the creative mind it works faster and harder to manifest the conditions in order to evoke more of the same emotion.

● ●

In order to manifest things consciously by the use of our will it is important to conceive of them clearly. Thoughts are living things. Be very clear about what it is that you are intending, be it action, experience, or material item. The key is to conceive, visualize, or otherwise experience an example of what it is you desire, and consciously place it in the subconscious mind whose roots are in the Universal Mind. Think of this example as an ethereal blueprint of what you would like to experience or have. Imagine that everything that exists in the material world has a blueprint or model in the Universal Mind. Everything seen has its roots in the unseen. It is this ethereal blueprint that we unconsciously use to create our experience. A Soul Warrior becomes an architect of consciousness, creating these blueprints with thought, awareness, and attention. This is the origin of the corresponding external thing we wish to manifest. Create a habit of seeing the blueprint as the real root of the things you experience in the world.

This is essential: the initial step to producing any external experience is the creation of a blueprint. Our thoughts unconsciously create these blueprints every day, the results of which are our daily lives.

The blueprint cannot form itself. This is the job of the conscious/deciding mind. The subconscious/creative mind is not the thinker or the decision-maker. Consciously create powerful intentions and visualizations, then release them to the infinite subconscious/creative mind and let it do the work! In the creative mind the model or seed acts like a magnet, attracting more and more energy that is associated with the image, until it manifests as an outside fact.

ethereal blueprint,
noun: a detailed plan of action, a celestial or spiritual seed or model

> "The nucleus (or seed of the prototype), once established is endowed with an unquenchable energy of attraction steadily increasing in power until the process of growth is completed."
>
> —T. TROWARD, The Edinburgh Lectures

Using the present tense in the mind and language is essential when constructing these visualizations. Creation works in the present tense. As you form your model, see it as though it already exists. If you imagine it as coming to you in the future, you perpetuate not having it now. The action/intention of mind or will plants this seed in the subjective mind and if allowed to grow undisturbed will eventually attract to itself all of the conditions essential to its manifestation in outward and visible form.

Your will is the most powerful force you have. The will is not the "might" of physical strength. It is the commanding energy of focus, attention, and intention. The will is like an internal laser beam that magnifies intention, subject, or emotion. What you focus on expands, and the will is the tool or force used to direct our focus and attention. We shine the spotlight of will on our desired result and use the power of will to keep out conflicting ideas.

It is important to understand that any opposing or doubting thought will cancel out the original intention and become its own bluprint that will attract its own results. Doubt creates conflicting energy that confuses your original intention. This is where the power of your will comes in. The will is not outward force, the will is power directed with attention and focus. Keep your attention on the desired result to the exclusion of any opposing thought process.

can you feel it?

The role of feeling and emotion in this most powerful process cannot be stressed enough. The way we *feel* about anything is what brings it into our lives. Our thoughts are externalized into the world through action and emotion. We can use our feelings as wonderful tools to manifest our deepest desires.

Though feelings and emotions may be labeled in a myriad of ways, there are really two main kinds of feelings: the ones that feel good and the ones that don't. These feelings can be used as a gauge to determine whether or not you are in alignment with the experiences you desire to have. If you think about something you want and it feels stressful or hopeless, then you are not in alignment, and those feelings will continue to manifest the opposite of what it is you want to experience.

When we have conceived of the item or experience that we would like to explore and we create our ethereal blueprint of it through visualization, we should strive to invoke every sense that we can. What would having this experience sound like, smell like? But most importantly, what does it feel like emotionally to have this experience? Does it bring joy, excitement, love, a thrill? The feeling or emotion creates a super thrust, an energy force that propels the manifestation of the desire. The most productive feelings for manifestation are enthusiasm and gratitude.

This works both ways—if you feel sad because you don't have something, the subconscious mind mirrors this and reflects sadness and lack back to you as your external experience. If you feel desperate for the seeming lack of money to pay your debt, the subconscious jumps on that feeling as an instruction and externalizes it as more desperation and seeming lack. Feeling anger on your side creates reactive anger on the other side. It creates distance between people. When someone who is angry feels judged for their anger they will either act out in more anger or repress their anger, creating shadows as a result of denying themselves expression.

This does not mean that we should not honor our feelings of anger, sadness, or desperation. Honor an emotion by feeling it when it arises, but do not hold onto it. Let it go. If you do not acknowledge that you have these feelings they will only externalize into your reality to get your attention. It is to your advantage to develop the skill of release and flow. It is powerful, not a weakness, to let any and every emotion flow through you without judgment or without trying to hold onto it. This even includes joyful emotions. If when we feel great we try to hold on tightly to the moment, we inhibit the flow of joy. Allow your emotions to flow like water through your experience. When you don't judge unhappy feelings you will transcend them without much effort on your part. The only effort you need apply is in taking care to not judge the feeling and to allow it to express itself.

> **"Any emotion that comes into awareness that is not fully experienced in the moment (or not released) is automatically stored in the subconscious. We often suppress them by escaping them. We take our attention off of them so we can push them back down."**
>
> **—HALE DWOSKIN, *The Secret***

When feeling any emotion you have the option to release it at will. We have a habit of holding on to our emotions, be they good or bad, trying to wring every last drop of feeling from them. There is no need to hold onto any emotion; it is much healthier to just let them flow through you. Being present to the emotion for a short time is enough; there is no preset time limit by which you should feel it. The point is to feel it fully so that it does not sit around in your system waiting for your attention. Once you are present to any emotion you can say, "I am present to this emotion and it is by my will that I release it from me," or anything that suits you, maybe something like, "peace and release." You can also transmute the energy of an uncomfortable emotion. Allow yourself to fully experience the emotion, then imagine filling yourself, or the emotion itself, with a golden light. This may help create a lighthearted feeling when you're feeling stuck or resistant to your situation.

> **"It is not what you are resisting that is causing the discomfort, it is the resisting that is causing it."**
>
> **—BILL HARRIS**

One thing we all need to come to terms with is that we are always responsible for the way we feel, no matter what we think someone else has done or how we have been treated by others. You are responsible for your feelings, actions, and reactions at all times. Every emotion is a valid form of life expression. Learn to express or release your emotions safely and without judgment. Inappropriate expression may lead to greater conflict. Your feelings are your own and it is not fair to project them onto others. Yodel, jump around, laugh uproariously, shake, scream, or punch pillows! Our emotions sometimes feel thick, heavy, and immovable, but in fact they have little substance and exist only on the surface like our thoughts, whereas peace and pure potential are the deep ocean that is the core of our being.

the world is yours . . .

All right, we now share a basic understanding of the process by which we grow our individual and collective lives. Let's put it all to work.

Sometimes when we try to think about what we really want to experience our desires can seem elusive. We all have things that we know we don't want to experience, so this is a good starting point. Begin by writing a list of up to five things that you know you do not want to experience, and if it is something you are all ready experiencing, put it on the list.

> **"The universe conspires to do your will."**
>
> **−DEEPAK CHOPRA**

WARRIOR WORKSHEET

List up to five things that you do not want to experience . . .

_____

_____

What are the opposites of these, things that you do want to experience?

_____

_____

Think about something you would like to bring into your life, be it something from the above list or something else entirely. Be *very clear* with the language you use. Writing it down is a good idea if you want to work with the wording (there is a glossary of affirmations on many subjects in the back of the book), Be very sure to word your intention in the present tense because the future is just a concept, but now is the eternal moment.

Each item or experience deserves your full attention. Do not overwhelm your conscious and subconscious minds with multiple requests at once. Take time with each desire, experiencing the feeling of having it in your visualization or meditation. If you have many things you are working to bring into your life, take one or two a day and set aside ample time for each of them to receive the attention they deserve.

WARRIOR WORKSHEET

Write about some things that you would like to experience or manifest. When you are clear about what it is you desire, write it in the form of an intention. Take your time. Play with the wording until you feel the words convey your intention properly. Remember, always word intentions positively and in the present tense.

FOR EXAMPLE:

I intend to accept myself and others as they are.

Select just one of the things you have listed. With the conscious mind, create and visualize the blueprint that you would like to impress upon the subconscious mind. Do *not* let your mind get caught up in "How is this gonna work?" When you are creating the blueprint do not concern yourself with *how*. To ask an infinite intelligence "how" only creates mental blockages in your own mind. "I really want this but I don't know *how* it will ever happen" or, "The only way this will ever happen is if this, this, and this happen first." When you sit there and try to figure out *how* to manifest your intention, you are actually setting up challenges (more blueprints) for your subconscious to manifest. The subconscious mind is seamlessly connected to the pure potential of the universe. Everything is possible, including instantaneous manifestation of your wildest dreams. When you worry about *how,* your mind actually figures out all the obstacles to your goals. The answer to *how* will be answered later. You may not immediately see the road to reaching your goal, but the eternal universe knows the best and fastest way to make anything happen. Let the universe show you how. Focus your will on the desired result. Keep your eye on the prize. Sometimes it's real hard, but you must trust. Concern yourself only with the desired result.

WARRIOR WORKSHEET

Now write down in as much detail as you can the thing or experience you wish to have. Describe colors, smells, sounds that are around you. Describe your emotions. How does it feel to have this experience or thing?

* * *

Once you have become clear about the details of your intention, ground yourself, bring yourself to a centered place of focus and then get into a state of visualization where you are experiencing as intensely as you can the actual feeling you would have when you attain your desired result. Once again, remember that feelings are very important as they are a physiological expression accompanying your thoughts. Emotions of any sort amplify the blueprint and give it added strength. Impress the image and emotion you want to manifest into the subconscious mind. Imagine it as if it exists now. What does it feel like in this instant?

For example, if you desire a fulfilling job or career, close your eyes and imagine what you might wear to such a job, what a day at work would be like, and especially how you feel doing this type of fulfilling work. Or if you desire to own a new home, close your eyes and imagine in as much detail as you can muster certain aspects of the home you wish to live in. "I live in a beautiful home with two stories, three large bedrooms, an enormous kitchen, a gorgeous green yard" and so on. Engage your senses and emotions in the visualization: "I can smell the food cooking in the kitchen, and I can hear the children playing outside. It feels so wonderful to live here."

GET YOURSELF COMFORTABLE. Now with the intention you have formed clearly in your mind, close your eyes and bring yourself into a state of meditation using whichever method you prefer. When you are relaxed and ready, create a clear mental picture or idea of what it is you intend to manifest. Experience this thing with the senses as if it already exists, for it does, within you. Allow yourself to feel the emotion associated with having this item or experience. Place the experience in the subconscious mind. One way to visualize this is to imagine the subconscious mind as a boat floating in the infinite ocean of the universe. Imagine you place the intention in this boat as it floats in pure potential. Say your intention out loud. Then say thank you to your subconscious mind for attending to this for you. When you are ready, open your eyes.

Write about this experience if you like.

Another effective technique that may be useful is to imagine your intention as a seed, and your subconscious as fertile soil. Plant the seed of your intention with words of love and a blessing, asking the subconscious soil to nurture the seed that it may grow and blossom to its full potential. Imagine the attention of the will is water, and whenever you think about your intention, visualize lovingly watering your seed/sprout/plant.

It's a good idea to create an affirmation or mantra about your intention. This will help keep the light of your will shining in the direction you want it to. Whenever you think about your intention in any way, especially if you are having doubting thoughts, you can say, think, or write your mantra repeatedly, as many times as you feel is effective, once or a hundred times.

FOR EXAMPLE:
> "I grow healthier every day."

These instructions and meditations are purely suggestions of methods you can use to bring the things and experiences you would like to have into your life. Take what works for you and leave what doesn't.

Write an affirmation in the present tense about your intention.

> "**Ask for what it is you desire with the same lightness as though you were asking someone to pass you a napkin, the secret is that you fully expect to get it!**"
>
> —IMURI

a formula

Another way to create an intention is by the use of a formula. The following is a formula you may use when forming an intention you would like to place into the subjective mind.

> **There is one** _____ *(Source, God, Divine Power, etc.),*
> **Which includes** _____ *(your intention—joy, love, moola),*
> **And I** _____ *(name)* **instruct my subconscious mind**
>   **to use this** _____ *(Divine Power, etc.)* **to manifest**
>   _____ *(your intention again),*
> **For the good of all and free will of all.**
> **And so it must be.**

FOR EXAMPLE:
> **There is one Source,**
> **Which includes abundance,**
> **And I, Pedro, instruct my subconscious mind to use this**
> **Divine Source to manifest abundance,**
> **For the good of all and the free will of all.**
> **And so it must be.**

When creating your intention, make sure that you are not trying to affect another's will. It will not help you to try to make someone go against their own will. These types of intentions will backfire negatively upon the intender. The words "for the good of all and free will of all" are there to ward against such intentions.

Write your intention using the formula on the previous page.

---

let's make moves . . .

You have now done the inner work required to experience your intention. Next it is time for the outer work. You must take the most natural step towards what it is you want to manifest. *This is so important!* You must move towards your desire. If it is a dream job, pick up the want ads and send in some résumés. If it is a new car, go take a test drive. If it is a lover, see a romantic movie and arrange a love altar (Chapter 12). Surround yourself with things that remind you of what it is you want to manifest, and whenever you remember, send positive energy towards your desired result, or use the power words. You *must take action.* The universe conspires to do your will, but you must be active so that the universe can present you with opportunities. As you go into the world taking steps towards your goals, opportunities will unfold one by one until your desire has externalized.

It is also necessary to take on an attitude of confident expectation. This means that you expect to have your desire unfold as much as you expect the sun to set tonight and rise tomorrow. Cultivating an attitude of confident expectation may take some practice. When feeling any doubt say your affirmation once or twice. Those who are successful at using these laws have a single-mindedness about attaining their goal, and this is the will in action, for nothing will stop them from having the experience that they have set their mind to. You make a decision and do not look back.

It is very important to realize that what you envision for your life may not happen exactly as you see it; the universe has infinite potential from which to manifest. When creating your intention use words like "this or something better manifests for me." Trust that the universe has your best interests at heart and that something even better can happen for you. Often plans do not materialize the way we had imagined, but they can be even more beneficial than anything we've ever dreamed up. Also make a choice to habituate yourself towards positive thinking, as it is the habitual thought process that creates a mental groove which, once established, needs little attention to produce the intended result.

WARRIOR WORKSHEET

What are some immediate actions you can take today, tomorrow, and in the coming weeks to actualize your intentions and desires?
JUST DO IT!

these are the tales of our lives . . .

A great tool for manifesting your desires is writing the *tale of your life*. This is a story of your life in the way you would like to see it. It does not matter whether you are a great writer, it doesn't matter how poetic it is, or how well it flows to the ears of others. This story is for you. You are creating a detailed and expanded version of a blueprint.

Tell it in first person, referring to yourself as "I," or tell it from a detached perspective as though you are telling the story about somebody else. Begin the story from your past or right now. Lay out your life story as you would like to experience it. Include as many different aspects of your life as you would like, or concentrate on one portion of your life and how you would like to see it unfold. This tale can be very helpful in helping you see things in more detail and from a broader perspective. Do this regularly if it becomes something you enjoy, or anytime there is a major change coming and you would like to lay some basic groundwork for how you would like events to play out.

• •

FOR EXAMPLE:

I am on a new life adventure! After doing the same work for over ten years I have decided to follow my dream of becoming a singer. I am moving to Los Angeles in three months. Between now and then I will have earned and received enough money to pay for the costs of the trip, plus rent and expenses for the first two months.

I will get rid of most of my belongings, taking only what I need. I look forward to being free from the material world for a while. I will rent a trailer to pull behind my car on the long road trip to L.A. I am so excited! When I arrive I will immediately find a gorgeous and afford-able apartment in a safe and lovely neighborhood. After settling in, I will immediately find or be offered employment. I will work thirty hours or less per week, and the rest of my time will be spent pursuing my goal. I will network with people in the music industry as often as possible. It feels so wonderful to be up in this mix. I trust that the universe will bring forth opportunities that will benefit me in the direction I intend to go. Throughout this experience I will meet wonderful people, some of whom will become my close friends. I joyfully surrender to the Source of life, knowing I will be protected and guided on my journey. I am open to receive the gifts and abundance of the universe.

This process is meant to lay the foundation and create a mental map of how you would like things to unfold. Add as many details as you can, and also make sure to include feelings in your descriptions. Once you have written your tale, you may do a visualization in which you imagine it as vividly as you can. Remember to not become too rigidly attached to the outcome of this tale. The universe may have a grander plan than you can even imagine, so be open to the pure potential and possibilities of the universe.

Write your own tale of a scenario you would like to experience. Get juicy with the details.

MENTAL
MORPHOSIS

programming, *verb:* to absorb or incorporate automatic responses or attitudes; to condition

WARRIORS, FOR A long time, our families, societies, and the powers that be have been mentally programming us to believe in the things that they want us to believe in. We have been programmed with ideas of beauty, fear, prosperity, lack, love, hate, mortality, and on and on. Changing or reprogramming the mental process is real work. We have been going at it the old way for a very long time and inertia has surely set in. But there is much hope, especially when you are dedicated to seeing and understanding the basic workings of the mind.

Take some time to examine the life you are currently creating. What are the patterns you see in your life? Can you see the cycles that seem to happen even when you try your hardest to change or avoid them? Deciding to reprogram your mental patterns starts with a long, hard look, a deep uncovering of how you are responsible for the circumstances you continually find yourself in.

The process of reprogramming is itself quite simple. It's all about repetition. It is repetition that has got you where you are today—repetition of ideals, standards, rules, and experiences. Repetition has embedded thought patterns into your mind, creating neural pathways for the thought impulses to move through effortlessly. You can create new pathways, new habitual thought patterns, which will effortlessly manifest the experiences you would like to have. The parts of us that believe in love attract more love. The parts of us that believe in lack repel prosperity.

As with the exercise from the last chapter, you may want to figure out first what is not working for you in your life and go from there. For some people it is helpful to dig deep into their memories to try to discover where their internalized messages originated from. For others, just knowing what to replace the old thought patterns with is enough. Once you know what it is you no longer want to encounter or experience, you can then reset your mind to experience other things.

When you know what it is that you want to reprogram, come up with an intention or affirmation to replace it. Whenever you see, hear, or feel the old programming at work, immediately recite your intention or affirmation.

Make a list of habitual ways of thinking, or other patterns or habits you would like to transform in your life. Consider each, one at a time, and come up with a corresponding affirmation in place of the old conditioning. Make a commitment to say this affirmation repeatedly throughout the day. Saying it in the morning as part of your rise and shine exercise is a great way to begin integrating it into your day. Writing the affirmation five to one hundred times is also a good way to begin reprogramming your thought process.

It is good to randomly say or write your affirmation throughout the day. But what is even more effective is to catch the thought patterns that you no longer want to have as they happen, and immediately replace these outworn ways of thinking with the new thought pattern.

what's the holdup?

We all have a deep subconscious system of beliefs that often hinders even the most active and positive attempts to manifest new things and ways of thinking. Our manifesting muscle has been busy repeating the same old thing for so long we really have to get into the active work of consciously creating to actualize some major changes. This is why visualization and getting into the *feeling* is so important. Smell the air, see the environment, hear the sounds, touch something—do all these things when using meditation and visualization. Call up each sense one by one and ask yourself, what do I smell, see, and so on. You've got to get your mind to *feel* what it's like to have what it is you are desiring, whether it is a trip to Kokomo or an escapade.

It is not unusual, even with all the attention you may be giving to your intention, that you are not truly in alignment with your desire. The subjective or subconscious mind stores all the memories of past experience and draws upon these memories first when reacting to any current thought, stimuli, or experience. These habitual ways of thinking and reacting are so embedded in our psyche that they need special attention in order to change or be reprogrammed. The subconscious has been running on autopilot for a very long time, which can be a good thing; it is your automatic manifesting instrument. The problem is that it is currently manifesting the same old shiz.

When something you are working to manifest seems to be taking a long time to externalize, there are several likely causes. Often it is because you have yet to *really* vibrate in a place of trust. It could be as simple as a matter of focus. Do you change what it is you desire quite often, for example: "I desire a beautiful relationship" versus "I am not really ready for a relationship right now"? If this is the issue, then more thought must be put into your intention. Is it truly what you want? Not just what you think you should want, or what you feel pressured to do? Also, beware of becoming impatient when the universe doesn't deliver on your schedule. It is not unusual to discover internal resistance within yourself, a lack of "allowing" in terms of how and when your desire will be fulfilled, which shows itself through your expression of impatience.

Let's look further at some hindrances and suggestions on how to deal with them.

> **"The temptation to quit will be greatest just before you are about to succeed."** —Chinese saying

timing

Often the divine timing is not right for the immediate manifestation. Some things take longer than others. Please be patient and allow time for things to line up in your life to make way for your desire to externalize. Time and space are constructs of the mind, and we often create a subconscious timeline in which things will happen. When we open ourselves to the opportunities that unfold around us they will lead us to our desires. It is our own ideas of worthiness, whether we truly believe we are deserving, that determine if and when something will manifest for us.

old patterns

Programmed behaviors and habits often override our true yearning for change. When old ideas are still influencing new desires you may not yet be in alignment with your conscious desire. Consciously or subconsciously you may be creating blockage that won't allow the desire to attract the proper circumstances.

For example, a person may be working on self-love regarding their body image. They may look into the mirror and say to themselves, "I am so beautiful, my body is so beautiful, and I love myself." But if for years and years prior to this work they have been saying to themselves, "I hate this body, I am so fat, no one will ever love me," then each time they try to work a positive affirmation, their subconscious may circumvent it with that habitual subconscious belief.

Your emotions are a wonderful gauge of whether or not you are in alignment with your desire. When you think about what it is you would like to attract, do you feel great and excited, or stressed and doubtful? If you feel stress or doubt when you think about experiencing your desire, you are out of alignment. It is time to do a meditation to clear your doubts or funk around your creative energy.

Do you feel out of alignment with that which you desire? Do you know what may be impeding the flow of your desired result? Write down whatever comes to mind.

clearing meditation/exercise

 CONSIDER WHAT IT IS you would like to bring into your life; love, peace, abundance, etc.

Sit quietly and concentrate on your breathing until you feel centered. Ground yourself if you wish. Ask yourself what experience or memory needs to be cleared so that you will be in better alignment with your desire.

Pay attention to any painful memories that arise. Follow them back as far as they go. Notice patterns in your past experience, behavior, or expectations. Look deeply for the roots of these issues. Any painful memories need to be cleared and others forgiven. The most important thing to be aware of are any feelings of guilt. Self-forgiveness is imperative in clearing the lines for manifestation.

To clear a memory, habit, or pattern, visualize it as clearly as possible, following it as far back as you can, to its inception if possible. Allow yourself to feel any emotion associated with the memory. Oftentimes our inability to feel emotion at the time of the original experience is the reason the memory gets stuck and is still able to affect us. It wants your attention. If you like, write about these memories, or about old emotional blocks you may have found in your energy field. Expand on them as much as you like. Connect the dots in your life and notice how this memory or experience has affected you in your life prior to this moment.

If you are unsure about the source of the impediment, use the above clearing exercise to define it more clearly. Gently trace the roots of the blockage as deep as you can. Is it an issue of worthiness? Do you feel that you don't deserve it? Did something happen associated with this particular object or experience that is specifically in conflict with having what it is you desire? Consider closely what you feel is in need of some special attention for transformation to come about. Reflect on what it is in you that may inhibit your current desire from becoming part of your present reality.

Say out loud (or in your mind):

> "I release you *(anger, guilt, pain . . .)*; I
> forgive you_____*(name)*; I forgive
> myself for . . ."

If you are using a grounding cord or root, you may send these memories down this cord into the Earth. Ask the Earth to recycle these energies into fertile beautiful flowers, that they may not affect you or anyone else negatively again.

It is very important, once you have cleared emotions and memories, to imagine light and/or love filling the places that have been cleared. If we forget to fill these places with light and love it is easier for that negativity to come right back and fill them up.

Subconscious training and reprogramming are often necessary to make changes in our hidden and unhealthy belief systems. Sometimes we need to identify shadows that have been left out of sight, avoided, or ignored. When we shine light on these shadows we are able to heal and integrate parts of ourselves that need our attention and love.

open to receive?

Another reason for the lag in the ability to attract your experience is sometimes an inability to receive. We spend so much time giving, or judging others for having, that we haven't created the ability to receive. We simply don't open our arms wide and accept the gifts life offers us. Does the idea of receiving something wonderful make you feel guilty in any way? Are you a person who has a hard time asking anyone for anything, whether it is a ride to work or a stick of gum? This can often be a deep-rooted self-worth issue. The ability to accept and receive is an essential technique for creating, manifesting, and attracting an experience or material object to you.

Meditate upon the thing you wish to attract: love, courage, power, money, health, enlightenment. Say to yourself, I accept this. Realize it is an extension of you. What about the responsibility that goes along with what you are drawing into your life? Take a moment to think about what it means to have what you want and what comes along with it. If you want to be a movie star, are you ready to accept that people, especially children, will look up to you and use your life as an example? Are you ready to accept the responsibility that goes with whatever you are bringing into your life? Find joy in the idea of having what it is you desire. Let your heart feel that joy. If this does not come naturally to you, make a concerted effort to visualize and really imagine the feeling of joy as a result of receiving your gift.

Bring yourself to a centered place and when you are ready say to yourself, either out loud or in thought, "I am open to receive and accept the blessings and abundance of the universe."

COSMIC LOVE

THE MOST WONDERFUL, succulent, and juicy thing we can experience here in this earthly realm is love. Love is our true essence; it is the life flowing through our body. There are many who would say that the word love cannot describe this life-giving, nurturing, supportive energy. And this may be true—love in modern society has come to describe infatuation, codependence, and conditional love.

Love is the most powerful force: it is with love for ourselves and others that we are able transform. It is the illusion of being without love that causes suffering. The concept of lack serves the illusion of suffering.

When you have made love a priority in your life by first loving yourself, you will find a certain peace of mind within your life. When you have a true appreciation of yourself, you will realize that you are supported in all your endeavors. Success and failure both serve to bring understanding and growth. Expanding your consciousness of love allows you to become a channel for the infinite flow of love.

i love you, but . . .

The love and appreciation of your own being will be a powerful indicator of the quality of all your other relationships. Your love for yourself will be a direct reflection of the relationships in your life. Any relationship in your life characterized by suffering is an indication that something within you needs attention. You are not responsible for other people's feelings or behaviors, but there is something *you* can do about *your relationships*. It all starts with you.

> "Learn how to carry a friendship greatly, whether or not it is returned. Why should one regret if the receiver is not equally generous? It never troubles the sun that some of his rays fall wide and vain into ungrateful space, and only a small part on the reflecting planet. Let your greatness educate the crude and cold companion. If he is unequal, he will presently pass away; but thou art enlarged by thy own shining." —RALPH WALDO EMERSON

There will likely be some people in your life who you don't understand or you just don't get along with. We all vibrate at different frequencies, and this is normal. It is up to you to decide how you feel and act in the presence of others. It is up to you not to take other people's words and actions personally. When you do get upset because you feel you have been wronged or hurt, take a minute to reflect how you are also responsible for the situation. The most important thing we can do within our relationships with others is grow and love. The things that happen in relationships, good and bad, are there to show us something about ourselves. When we can experience each of our relationships with an open heart and without judgment our capacity to love grows tremendously.

The key to love is acceptance. Most of us love ourselves and the people in our life as much as we know how. But if we looked at each relationship one at a time we may be surprised at the conditionality of our love. We love someone when they do right by us and give us the attention and nurturing we want that feeds our ego. But when this person does something we don't approve of, or isn't as attentive as we would like, we withdraw our love. This is conditional love—"I love you if . . ." or "I love you, but . . ." Unconditional love takes some deep reflecting upon one's self, uncovering the unreachable expectations we have for others, and often a realization that our love is conditional because we don't feel whole. When your concern is that you are not receiving enough love, you have also found the answer—you are not giving yourself the love you deserve and so are falling short in your relationships.

We all long to be loved, and sometimes withhold our love from others if we feel we are not receiving our fair share. This is stingy loving. If you can learn to love unconditionally you will be loved unconditionally, by yourself, by friends, family, and lovers, and by the entire universe. The universe loves you unconditionally anyway. The universe holds nothing back from you, it gives you what you think about and what you feel, no matter what it is. The more you think and feel, the more you receive what it is you are thinking about and feeling, whatever it is. The universe doesn't put conditions on giving to you. What you ask for, either consciously or unconsciously, you will receive. It does not judge your decisions as good for you or bad for you because it knows everything you experience will lead you back to your true self at some point in your experience.

> "Your task is not to seek for love, but merely to seek and find all the barriers within yourself that you have built against it."   —UNKNOWN

When loving someone or something, love it without condition. When your love is given with the desperate energy of doing so in order to receive (love given with conditions), your true intention is exposed. Your higher self can't be fooled. You will experience love as elusive if you're only putting energy out to *get*. Love flows to you effortlessly all day long, it flows into you by the very act of breathing. When you feel you are in need of love, bring your attention to the breath and feel gratitude for this life. This is receiving love.

When you want to give love to others the method is simple—outflow. To outflow is to visualize or otherwise become aware of loving energy coming from you or through you out to a particular person, to humanity, or to the universe. Visualize love energy coming from your heart. You can imagine the person or persons to whom you want to give love standing in front of you, and see them full of joy and bathed in radiant white light. Or you can simply say, "I send loving energy to (so and so)." If you want to send your love out to all life, just intend it, say it out loud, or imagine white light saturating everyone and everything.

WARRIOR WORKSHEET

freely giving love to others

Write about someone whom you feel you are loving conditionally. When you acknowledge that you sometimes love conditionally, you can choose to heal your relationships by opening your heart and loving freely.

vibing, *verb*: to
experience
harmonious
vibrations with
other persons
or things

Bring yourself to a quiet state of centeredness or meditation. Visualize someone or something (the Earth, a tree, or your home) that you would like to outflow love to. Imagine this being bathed in white or golden light. Or you may visualize a green light (the color of the energy emitted from the heart chakra) like a laser beam coming from your heart and connecting to the heart of the other. This exercise is to be done without expectation, without a desire of some action on the part of the other in regards to you. If the other person is in alignment with the receiving of unconditional love, they will be able to receive the love, though not always consciously. Your own energy will feel wonderful merely by being a conduit for love to flow through.

look at the bright side . . .

Warriors, we all have relationships that we believe could use some improvement. Some are with people we love, live with, or see every day. Some are with family members or old friends. Sooner or later one or more of these relationships is going to hit a rough patch, or maybe it already has. Has a certain relationship always had a low-level undercurrent of difficulty? We do not all vibrate at the same frequency at the same time, there are going to be times when our personalities don't gel with each other or we just completely clash.

If we find that the underlying tension has become the norm of any relationship, there are things we can do to address the situation. If you find that disagreements and arguments are happening more and more, or if you are living with a daily resentment of someone in your life, consider the following ways to explore the problem.

Take a few moments and think about the person you are not vibing with. Make a list of the traits or issues that you are feeling resentful about or are irritated with.

Do you see these traits in yourself? Really take a moment to consider your role in the way these interactions happen. Are you a victim in this experience? Are you constantly expecting the other to act in a way you do not approve of, and they fulfill that expectation? Are your expectations of this person unreasonable? *What does being irritated about this situation say about your understanding, acceptance, or personality?*

Now make a list of the positive aspects about this person.

When you next come into contact with this person, be it on the phone, Internet, or in person, say some positive things about him or her, out loud or in your mind. Or say something positive about the interaction you are about to have.

When you do this you create a warm and inviting place for the vibrations that you appreciate about the other person to express themselves. The other person cannot be difficult around you if you have created a peaceful vibration. And if through sheer determination on their part they are still being negative, you, having created a peace shield around your aura, are unaffected by their attitude. Either they will feel the need to leave your presence, or you will be drawn away.

You can also create a positive affirmation about the relationship. This can reflect some positive aspect that already exists or something you would like the relationship to embody.

> "Human beings only learn and evolve through relationship. The only way we can see ourselves objectively is through the reflection of others. We can go off and sit in a cave and meditate for years, but we only really find out what happened in that cave when we come out and get involved with other people. So we need each other if we want to evolve."
> —ANDREW COHEN

soul contact

Because we are One, we have the ability to be in soul contact with anyone and anything at any moment. Time and space are but illusions of the mind. You are the center of All, so you can always reach out and touch someone with your soul. Soul contact is a great way to send love vibrations as well as to resolve conflict. The soul does not think at the level of the mind; it is not concerned with petty offenses and cannot be swayed by selfish ends. It can be a wonderful and pure space for communication between beings.

This technique can be used in a multitude of ways and for many reasons. When there is something you wish to convey to someone and are having a hard time doing it face to face, use soul contact. Or maybe you have had contact but it did not resolve the issue. Perhaps you just want to send someone some good energy and some love.

Let's say, for example, you are not getting along with someone at work, someone you barely know. Whenever you come into the office you feel snubbed by this person. Or on the positive side, you want to offer appreciation and love to your child's teacher. Soul contact is a nice way to have a peaceful interaction at the level of the soul.

● ●

Start by bringing yourself to a centered place. This can be within meditation or with just a few deep breaths and concentrated thought. Speak first to your soul-self, informing it of your intention to connect with this other being. Your soul already knows your intentions, but this is good for clarification within your own mind. When you are ready, call to the person with whom you want to have soul contact, say or think, "Soul of _____ I speak to you from the ethereal level of the soul (or the level of all life, or of love, etc.)." From this place you can convey, either by saying it out loud or by thinking, whatever message you would like the other person to receive. Realize that the soul of the other cannot be moved by your will, and any intention on your part to affect another's will can only backfire. You cannot make somebody act like you want them too. But you can say that you would like to have peace with this person, and that you would like to offer them love or forgiveness. The other soul is above the personality issues of its person; it is not angry at or judgmental of you; it will not laugh at your efforts. You are making an attempt to harmonize your frequency with another. The effort itself on your part will affect you, even if it is not discernable. By making the decision to go to someone on the level of the soul, you have already transcended the issue.

Can you think of any relationship in your life that could benefit from some soul contact? Write down what that conversation might sound like.

---

holding space

Do you know what it means to hold space for someone, or to have someone hold space for you? It is a simple and profound way to show love, support, and acceptance. Friends, colleagues, and loved ones will often come to you with their heart-aches, problems, complaints, and pain. They also come with their excitement and joy.

When someone comes to you with their concerns, it is very powerful when you can hold space for them. This means allowing them to express whatever they need to. Your role in holding space is to listen attentively, without interruption and without judgment. Allow the other to say and feel whatever is on their mind and heart. This may be accompanied by an emotional outburst. Often the person just needs to say these things out loud so that they can process the information. But sometimes they are looking for your advice, or they want you to validate their feelings in some way so that they can feel like they are right. In these cases use love as your reference point.

Sometimes you may feel that you need someone to hold space for you. It is okay to ask for it. If the other person is not familiar with the term, explain it simply as attentive listening without judgment. The power of holding space allows the person who is communicating their experience to do so without fear of judgment, allowing for a more honest expression of their feelings. This honesty often leads the person to their own resolution of the issue.

LOVE THANG

THE EXPERIENCE OF intimate love is something many of us long for. There is something special about sharing your mind, body, and soul with your beloved, something amazing about being accepted and honored for who you are right now. There is power within a partnership, where you feel you are in it together, come rain or shine.

The quality of your intimate relationships are bound up in the quality of your personal relationship with yourself. In a powerful and supportive relationship, one grows to love themselves even more as they experience love with another. There are challenges to face in any relationship, and even more so with the person you are intimate with. Intimate relationships expose our deepest fears and our most painful wounds, having these shadows revealed is actually a blessing in disguise. One of the most important roles that our most cherished relationships play is to uncover these wounded parts of ourselves so they can be witnessed, loved, and healed. An authentic and empowered relationship will allow for you to share your doubts and fears so they can be nurtured and loved.

A real relationship, in which we can be our authentic self, both powerful and vulnerable, can be the most effective tool for growth. For what can be more important in our experience than love? In our society it is common for us to put our careers or goals first. There is logic, of course, to meeting your own needs first.

But be careful that love does not fall by the wayside, with the material world becoming all-important in comparison. The stuff of the world can never satisfy the way love can. Sharing a deep and profound love with another can bring deep wisdom, understanding, and ultimately transformation.

Being solitary, without an intimate partner, either by choice or circumstance, is also satisfying. Many of us choose not to be in a relationship for many reasons; we may prefer our own company, or prefer to not be intimate. Your life is whole and complete without the constant presence of anyone else. There is a divine fullness in your life when you love and nurture yourself, and fulfill your own needs.

Any relationship that you are a part of, whether platonic or romantic, exists for your emotional and spiritual growth, and for your friend or lover. Even the most dramatic and unhealthy relationships expose what we believe about ourselves that needs healing attention. Our love relationships serve as our greatest reflections. When we can find the gift in even the strangest of couplings we are able to overcome internal challenges and realize our wholeness.

> **"We are made for loving. If we don't love, we will be like plants without water."** —ARCHBISHOP DESMOND TUTU

gimme some sugar . . .

We can bring a loving relationship into our lives the same way we bring any other thing we desire into our lives—with attention. There are numerous people in the world who would be a great match for you. The soul-mate ideology creates a suggestion that there is one perfect love for you, and perhaps there is, but it is even more likely that there are many wonderfully compatible people with whom you can have a deep meaningful and spiritual connection.

Whomever you are attracting, and whoever is attracting you, is drawn to the particular frequency that you are emitting, and vice versa. As we change and grow our energy vibrations change and grow too, attracting frequencies that resonate with our own.

Any person, past or present, who you have had an intimate or love relationship with was perfect for you in terms of the growth and wisdom you needed to receive from the involvement. With love and attention each person can choose to grow and expand until they become aware of the continuous flow of love that moves though them. When we truly honor ourselves as connected with the divine, the relationships we find ourselves in will mirror that understanding, and that glory.

Many of us also have an imaginary ideal that we think our love relationships should look like. You think the person that is your soul mate will look a certain way and act a certain way, and once you find each other everything will be peachy keen. This is unrealistic. Even the most ideal of relationships experience some form of conflict. The expectations some of us have created in the form of a hypothetical man or woman are often so unreal, like a fairy tale. We can get so caught up in the hypothetical that the person with whom we could have a wonderful relationship may be standing right next to us and we don't see them. These unreal expectations are usually born of a feeling of incompleteness that no one can ever fill. Or else we create relationship criteria so high that there is no risk of someone meeting our standards, and thus no chance of getting hurt.

An ideal, healthy relationship consists of two people of any gender who are willing to love and accept each other completely, and are able to be individuals within the relationship. You are a whole being and your partner is a whole being. She cannot complete you, you cannot fix him. Building an authentic and enduring love relationship takes time and effort from both parties. It takes a genuine willingness to accept that at times there will be conflict, and a determination to honor each other through the process of healing.

The magic of love is that it continues to expand. Your heart just continues to grow and there is more and more capacity for more love. The feeling place gets deeper, and acceptance and understanding grow exponentially. Our concept of love is just a drop in the bucket of what love really is.

If you are ready to be involved in a powerful and loving partnership there are fun ways to draw love to you. The first step begins, of course, with a deep appreciation and love for yourself. Without this basic ingredient, every relationship will eventually be found lacking. When you come into a relationship as a whole and complete being, the people who are drawn to you will also have an understanding of their wholeness. From this place you can create an interdependent relationship. This differs greatly from a codependent relationship. A codependent relationship is a mutually dependant relationship, where each person does not feel complete on their own and looks to the other person to complete them. Our society is infused with codependent messages from media: songs that say things like, "I can't live without you" or "I am nothing without you;" soap operas, primetime dramas, and movies that promote codependency and call it love. Interdependency is when two individuals contribute to the relationship and complement each other. People in healthy relationships depend on the sharing of responsibilities, but do not collapse themselves into the relationship; they still recognize themselves as individuals.

so, whadd'ya want?

We all have an idea floating around in our mind of what kind of person we would like to share our life with. But unless you take some real time and give this topic serious thought it is likely that the person you attract will end up without the traits that are most important to you. If you don't really know what is important to you in a partnership you may attract a person who doesn't resonate with your ideas, or lifestyle. What do you feel is essential to have in a relationship? Humor, romance, kindness, sensuality?

Bring your desires from deep in the recesses of your mind out into the physical reality by writing a list of the most important characteristics you want in a relationship without creating unrealistic ideals of perfection. Realize that you can't go to the extreme and create a partner from scratch—you don't want a Frankenstein. There always will be some surprises in the lover you attract.

WARRIOR WORKSHEET

Make a list of five to ten of the most essential things that you desire in a relationship. This is important, so take your time to consider them.

Now make a list of up to another ten or so things you would like to have in a relationship that won't make or break the relationship for you. This can include physical characteristics. These things are not imperative to the relationship, but it would be nice to have them.

Now write a list of at least ten attributes you have that you can bring to a relationship. Yes, you. We have all these ideas about what we would like to get out of a relationship, but we rarely consider or appreciate what we may have to offer to a loving partner.

---

ethereal lover

Now that you have a solid understanding of what you want in a relationship, you can do some soul-contact interacting with your love. Begin by bringing yourself into a state of meditation. When you are ready to begin the soul-contact, imagine that your love is sitting in front of you. As of yet, you do not know what this person looks like, and you should keep it that way. Do not create a mental image of your love, for this limits the possibilities; the love that is coming to you may not arrive in the package you are expecting. See your love sitting before you, but as a shadowy picture. Call to the soul of this being although you do not yet know this person. Express your love for him or her, have gratitude that this being is coming into your life, and express your readiness to experience a healthy loving and spiritual relationship. Imagine green light radiating out of your heart and into theirs, and green light radiating out of his or her heart into yours. Or if you prefer, imagine that the being in front of you is bathed in white or golden light, and although you cannot see their face you can feel their joy.

Speak to your love throughout the day or during any meditation, expressing love and patience, letting them know you are ready to experience this union.

Sexual energy is a very powerful energy that can be created between two people, or can be created with oneself through masturbation. Fantasies involving love making between you and your lover can strengthen the bond as well as intensify the magnetism between you. Visualize yourself and the shadowy figure, your lover, making beautiful love. Do this while pleasing and stimulating yourself sexually. Imagine that you are giving your partner intense pleasure, and that you are receiving intense pleasure from your partner. Feel your heart radiate love for this wonderful person. Bring yourself to orgasm and as you climax say to him or her, "I love you." Imagine that the powerful, loving energy you have released moves out into the universe and envelopes your unknown lover.

Surrendering your attachment and expectations about who, when, and where you will meet this love is very helpful. If you are constantly wondering when you are going to meet this person, you are inhibiting the natural flow and order of this cosmic meeting. Surrender your desire to be in an intimate relationship to the universe, or the Source. Trust in the natural order of the universe to align you with your love at the right time. Accept that you don't know when or where this magical meeting will take place. Instead of concerning yourself with desire for your partner, use that energy to give to yourself the loving energy you would like to receive from another.

If you already have feelings for a specific person and are hoping to get their attention or to create a loving partnership with them, releasing attachment to the outcome will be more beneficial than clinging to the desire of being with this person. Surrender your desires to the universe, saying something like, "I desire to share a loving relationship with Martha. I release this intention into the universe." When we cling to a desire we are resisting the natural ebb and flow of circumstances. Right now you and this person do not have the relationship that you desire to have. Accept what is, state your desire to the universe, and release or surrender. Or you can say, "I desire to share a loving relationship with Martha, or someone with whom I would be wonderfully compatible." The universe is infinitely wise; the person you have chosen as the object of your affection may not be in alignment with your spiritual or evolutionary needs. Releasing attachment opens up the endless potential for someone to enter your life that would suit your current understanding.

sacred love space . . .

You may choose to create a sacred love space or love altar to honor love and to draw love. You may use the altar that you have already created, or start a fresh one just for this purpose. This altar is dedicated to the essence of love. If you are using your original altar, make a bit of room for the love space. A love altar consists of things that remind you of love or that you feel honor the essence of love. This can be fresh flowers (fresh only), a romantic postcard or something with powerful, loving, or sensual words or symbols on it. It can have figurines that are kissing, hugging, or engaged in some sexual pose. Rose crystal vibrates and attracts love. A picture or symbol that represents you is a good thing to have because love starts with you and you don't want to leave yourself out of the equation.

If you are already in a relationship, the two of you can create and supply items and energy for an altar to honor the love you share. Both partners can contribute to maintaining the freshness of the altar. If you are drawing love into your life, put your list of attributes on the altar. Light a candle or incense to celebrate all the love you already have in your life as well as the love you are drawing into your life.

messages of love

In Chapter 6 we wrote love letters to ourself as a way to appreciate and turn our loving energy back upon ourselves. It is also fun to write love letters to the lover whom you are attracting. This is a way to express your feelings, desires, hopes, and dreams. It is also a way to express your fears. If you are in a love relationship, write a letter to your love, expressing things you might not usually say. You can give it to him or her, put it on your altar, or keep it for yourself as a reminder of your love for him or her.

MESSAGES OF LOVE . . .

LOVE GROOVE

LOVE BETWEEN TWO people who deeply respect, honor, and care about each other is a supreme manifestation of the Source. Our love for our partner brings out the best and worst parts of ourselves. Often, being with another allows us to go deeper into our potential, and to love beyond the boundaries of what we thought love was. Being loved for your authentic self is the greatest gift, and it is also the greatest challenge. Love is the building block for all relationships—it is with love that we grow, heal, and explore our divine and mysterious selves and partners.

Soul Warriors are learning to be sincere in their service to their partners and are learning the meaning of unconditional love. When you are balanced within your own life, you are able to expand and allow love to flow through you unselfishly. Though we all have moments of judgment and fear, a sacred love shared with another is a vessel to carry you both to the shore of deep acceptance and understanding. A relationship is an ongoing challenge; there are times of great joy and peace, times of stagnancy, and times of conflict. These tides of emotion and change are reflections of your inner journey and will always serve your highest growth. Within the comforts of a loving, intimate relationship both partners are honored for their basic humanity. The process of opening the heart is a practice of surrender. This is not a surrendering to the will of another, but surrendering to love and all it has in store for you.

There are no guarantees but one, an opportunity to grow in service, compassion, and acceptance for yourself and others.

Your relationships are here to serve you and your partner in many ways, and there are no preset terms or limits to the length of any given relationship. Our society tries to tell us we should be with our love till death do us part. This is crap. You should be with your partner for as long as you both are able to be in loving service to the other, and are able to grow independently and as a couple. When the relationship is no longer serving you or your partner in terms of love and growth, then the relationship may have come to its limits. Some couples will make extraordinary efforts to reconcile a relationship, and this often has successful results; something new and wonderful is often produced in times of extreme emotion that will bring new life to a relationship, allowing it to endure. Tremendous healing can occur within a loving and nurturing relationship. But for others, no matter how they try they are unable to overcome conflict in the relationship. Often in these situations partners must leave the relationship to begin to heal. If this is so, be grateful for a new opportunity to be free of the constant influence of someone whose energy is not in harmony with yours. Rejoice that you will begin anew on a path of self discovery.

> **"Love is the magician that pulls man out of his own hat."**
>
> **—BEN HECHT**

so this is love??

We have all been in relationships that start with sparkly feelings of "this is the one!" The phase that has been called *infatuation* is a special time when each person sees God or the Source in the other, each person feels love's potential, and gives love in a selfless way. But within the first few weeks or months as we become more familiar with our new partner, we begin to see traits in them that we may not completely accept, and they will have similar issues with us. You notice things that you either don't like or you feel need some tweaking. You may fear the other person isn't giving you the attention and love that you desire, and so you begin the game of withholding love and affection instead of giving love freely without expectation of what you will receive.

> "The beginning of love is to let those we love be perfectly themselves, and not to twist them to fit our own image. Otherwise we love only the reflection of ourselves we find in them."
> —THOMAS MERTON

Once you are in a place of trying to get love from the other, the synergy within the relationship changes form. You have gone from giving love freely to now desperately trying to get it. Before, when you were giving it freely, so was your partner, but now, as you try to *get*, the natural flow is impeded. When you give love freely to yourself and others you will also receive it; you will receive it from yourself, and through many other sources in the universe (one of which could be your partner). Receiving is different than getting. To receive something, it must first be offered by someone who is giving. To try to get something from someone before it is offered is more like taking. You may always receive love freely from the universe. Give love fully to yourself, and to your love, without expectation of a certain result. If you are wondering how to give love, imagine a green light from your heart is streaming into theirs, or see them joyfully surrounded in white or golden light. Surrender to the love you share with this person, surrender and release, all will unfold as it should.

One thing you can always count as a good indicator of the quality of the relationship is whether or not you feel like you can accept

GIVE LOVE . . .

- ▶ Take the lead and plan something fun for the two of you, handling all the details such as babysitting.

- ▶ Get your love a special treat from the grocery store, without them asking for it.

- ▶ Give them a small trinket or symbol of your love.

- ▶ Run them a hot, candlelit bath complete with soft tunes and a glass of wine.

- ▶ Buy them a massage or weekly class they would enjoy. Go together?

- ▶ Make a special dinner in their honor, just the two of you, or invite a couple of close friends.

- ▶ Meet for lunch and bring him or her one beautiful flower (please remove plastic wrapping!).

- ▶ Get away for the weekend, drive to the next town. Or rent a room in a luxury hotel in your own town, stock up on wine and treats, and enjoy each other . . . thoroughly.

- ▶ Write a love letter or find a beautiful card and send it in the mail.

- ▶ Create a love altar together; explain the significance of each object to each other.

this person right now exactly the way they are. It is very common to fall in love with the potential of the other person or relationship. We can all see the potential that exists in others. But the other person may or may not reach the potential you see for them. It is even more likely that they will continue to be exactly as they are right now for a long while; change most often happens slowly and cannot be forced with good results. So, can you accept him or her, exactly as they are right now? If not, you have some soul searching to do. Either this person is not the right person with which to have a relationship with right now, or you need to find a genuine acceptance for who this person is, even if they never change.

● ●

When you can love someone completely without trying to possess them, you are on the right track. To possess someone is to want to know where they are every minute of every day; to feel like the other cannot be trusted; to feel like you can't be without them. Jealousy is a possessive trait. If you feel like you are or have been in a relationship in which you felt possessed by the other, or like you wanted to possess the other, do some reflecting on why. Often it is a feeling of incompleteness that makes us want to possess or be possessed by another.

Be aware of any judgment you have about yourself. Take care to release these false ideas about yourself, or you will transfer that judgment into your relationships. If we can accept ourselves for who we are we can genuinely be accepted by our partners for who we are, and accept them in turn. Accepting others for who they are is an ongoing theme. You may be able to accept him or her right now, but will you be able to do so next week? If you are in a relationship, and want to continue being in the relationship, add acceptance to the *rise and shine* exercise from Chapter Six. Or throughout the day say to yourself, "I accept Matilda exactly as she is right now."

Sharing your feelings of appreciation and love for the other verbally, even if it makes you somewhat uncomfortable, is imperative.

Few of us read minds, so although you may think your feelings for your partner are well known, you may be surprised at the profound effect simple words of love can have on any relationship. The actions you take to show your love are wonderful as well. A healthy relationship requires both loving words and loving actions to express one's deep feelings. The effect for the person on the receiving end will be to value your words and actions beyond what you can understand.

WARRIOR WORKSHEET

Consider your relationship. When was the last time you expressed your appreciation for your love? What did you say or do?

What do you appreciate now about your lover and your partnership? Can you express these feelings to him or her? Does the idea of sharing your feelings feel overwhelming? Explore why.

Make a list of a few things you can say and do over the next few days to show appreciation and love for your partner.

_____

Make a list of the things your partner could do or say to show appreciation for you. Do you feel comfortable expressing these things to your partner? Why or why not?

_____

work it!

Whether you are already in a love relationship or desiring to attract one, be firm in your resolve to do the work. Being in a healthy loving relationship takes responsibility. First and foremost there is a responsibility to be true to yourself, to take time for yourself, and to make sure you are not leaving yourself out of the equation in regards to giving to yourself. There are responsibilities that go with being a loving partner, which include being willing to communicate and listening to communications; being open and nonjudgmental with your partner; and sharing the responsibilities of living together and raising children, even if the children aren't yours.

Just like a plant that will die without the nurturing energy of the sun and water, every relationship needs attention and love to survive. When you have been in a relationship with someone for awhile you may notice one or both of you taking the relationship for granted. Or you may see patterns you have created within the relationship that may not be healthy, or may even be detrimental to a long term relationship. There are many of you out there who are in partnerships and are wondering how much longer you can put up with the way things are going. Something needs to change.

We tend to focus most of our attention on the things about the relationship that we do not necessarily agree with or like. The situation at issue could be anything; lack of communication or constant arguing. Whatever it is, if the relationship is full of love and if it is important for you to see it through as far as you can, then it is time for some work.

The first thing to do is acknowledge the positive aspects of this relationship. Sometimes we become fixated on the negative aspects of a relationship and forget to acknowledge the beautiful things about the person we love. Realize that if you have issues with the relationship that it is equally likely your partner does too. These things may or may not have already been communicated. Consider things in the relationship that *you* could improve upon that would bring peace and receptivity. This could be as simple as saying "I love you" more often, or doing the dishes once more a week. It is so crucial for us to realize that improving a relationship is a two-way street; we may need our partner to work on some issues, but we most likely have our own work cut out for us as well. If you feel like there is nothing that you need to do to fix the relationship, that it is all your partner's fault that things are falling apart, you need to check yourself.

Resolve to make your partner feel more loved; say sweet things to her, make slow delicious love to him. And do this without expectation for something in return. We must do this simply because we *love* them. You can't go around buying your partner things like a fancy piece of jewelry or a big-screen TV, thinking, "This is sure to get me more sex"—love is not for sale!

One of the roles of an intimate partnership is to expose buried wounds that need healing. There is nothing like a relationship to remind you of all the hurts and fears of the past. This is a very powerful situation. If you can be attentive to the different feelings that come up in you, they will heal. A powerful and enduring partnership is one in which you can share these feelings of insecurity without fear of judgment, and you can also hold space for your partner's hurts and fears.

WARRIOR WORKSHEET

What do you desire to experience in your relationship?

Write down several positive attributes about your partner.

Write down the thing or things you feel are lacking or are issues within your relationship.

FOR EXAMPLE:
We argue all the time over stupid things.

Now, write a positive statement or affirmation to replace the old one.

FOR EXAMPLE:
We can heal our relationship by communicating in a loving and respectful manner.

Now that you have an affirmation that reflects the issue in a different light, use it often. You are just as responsible as your partner. Whenever you find a negative about your partner in your thought process, find the corresponding positive and say it until the original thought has left your mind space.

Now, of course there are exceptions to this. If you are being abused, blatantly underappreciated, dishonored, and disrespected on a regular basis, you must do some heavy reflecting on yourself. These situations are very unhealthy and could have repercussions for you in the long term. You are the Source! You must know it even if your partner does not. Do what is in *your* highest good—and that may mean leaving the relationship for good. Don't sell yourself short. You are worth the love that you can imagine for yourself.

juicy power . . .

Sexual energy is one of the most potent and powerful forces that we have access to. In its highest manifestation it is pure, undiluted energy. It can be a path to love, healing, and to the Source of All. Of course, this is not always true, and happens according to the consciousness of those involved in the sexual encounter. The bliss of sexual pleasure has the potential to transcend the ego, or, on a more base level, to temporarily fulfill the ego.

Sexual intercourse is a sacred act, and was revered in ancient cultures. There were entire rituals centered on the act of sex. These ceremonies celebrated the divine act of creation. The male organ symbolized active and potent energy, and the female organ signified fertility and receptivity. Together this union symbolized the merging of duality into one. Only in the last few hundred years has sex and sexuality been dishonored and called dirty and sinful in an effort to bring shameful feelings to this sacred practice. Many religions have tried to instill an idea that sex is in opposition to spirituality.

● ●

Sex is a sacred place where two souls meet without the normal inhibitions found in daily life. Sacred sex is about more than sharing physical pleasure from our bodies: it is about sharing and exchanging the energy of the soul. When two beings are wrapped up in a passionate and sensual act or embrace they often lose the mask of ego and are able to be their authentic selves, even if only for a few moments.

> "Put away your pointless taboos and restrictions on sexual energy—rather help others to truly understand its wonder, and to channel it properly."
>
> **—NEALE DONALD WALSH**
> **God, channeled by Neale Donald Walsh**

Sexual energy has the capacity to be an intense and immensely powerful tool for transformation and healing. You can generate this energy with yourself or with a partner. Sexual energy, when used with conscious intention, has the power to affect our daily existence. Practicing sacred sex is as simple as honoring the divine within yourself and your partner in your intention, or with words and caresses, taking time in the process of slow, sweet lovemaking, looking deep into each other's eyes, or requesting what you desire from the other without fear.

The energetic power generated in sacred sex can be directed to serve us in the creation of our daily lives. When one uses the power of intention and then sends the intention out with the vibrational power of climax or orgasm, its potential is endless.

with self

BECOME YOUR OWN lover. Spend time alone getting comfortable with your body, experimenting and sensing your response. Making love with yourself can be very satisfying. Begin familiarizing yourself with these exercises by doing them alone; this way you can concentrate on the process without being concerned about your partner's role or pleasure. Consider very clearly what it is you are affirming or intending before you begin. Bring yourself to the edge of orgasm, and when you feel climax begin, clearly state the intention or affirmation out loud or in your mind. It may take a few tries to get the timing right because it does take focus and concentration to be able to direct your mind to the intention at the right time. Realize that the energy is being released with pure power into the universe.

For body-temple work, tighten or clench the muscles so that all of the powerful energy is directed inside when you climax, instead of being released out into the ether. As the waves of orgasm wash over you, say healing intentions or affirmations such as, "I love myself," "I am whole," or "I revitalize all of my organs." Imagine you are filled with all the awesome creative and healing energy you have just brought forth. This definitely takes practice, as we are in the habit of releasing control of these muscles at this point rather than contracting them. This type of exercise is also very good for men who are learning to control their ejaculation.

> **"Spiritual sex is best practiced with yourself or an uncon-ditionally loving and willing partner. To be able to trust and surrender to your partner or yourself is essential as the aim is to soften separation boundaries and emotion-al amour with selfless and sharing intentions."**
>
> **—CAROLINE ROBERTSON**

with a partner

THIS EXERCISE IS best used by loving couples who feel open enough with each other to take their sexual relationship to the next level. Imagine you and your partner with open hearts breathing together, pleasuring each other, and surrendering together into the bliss of love. To do the work together you must first discuss and decide on a shared intention. During the sexual act think about the intention, remind each other of it, talk gently about it. The point is not to forget the intention as the sexual energy builds. The more ecstatic the feelings, the more the mind empties (which is great because the intention has access to so much more power as there are fewer thoughts in the mind at this time). Attempt to climax together, although we know this does not always occur simultaneously. If the woman climaxes first she must say the intention out loud or state it in her mind. As she does this, the man also holds the intention in his mind. Then as he climaxes, he says the intention as she holds the intention in her mind. Of course the impact is twice as great if you can climax together.

PROLIFIC PROFITS

THE WORD *abundance* has a feeling of overflowing fullness. Acknowledging and having gratitude for the abundance in your life will bring you a sense of fullness, and will inevitably attract more bounty to you. We live in an infinite universe; there is an unlimited supply of abundance available to us at all times. We are only limited by our preexisting thought patterns about what we can and should have or not have. Abundance can be experienced on so many levels. Sharing love with family and friends is abundance. Experiencing beautiful moments and experiences in your daily life, such as the scent and grace of a lovely flower, are other forms of abundance. Abundance isn't something to get, it is innate within us and only has to be recognized.

True abundance involves experiencing harmony in the fundamental aspects of your spiritual life, emotional life, physical life, relationships, and financial life. Consider for a moment each of these aspects of your life. Do they feel abundant to you? You have the ability to bring abundance to your life simply through your thoughts, feelings, and actions.

loot, bread, funds, bucks, dough, dinero, chips, scratch . . .

Money, baby! We're all trying to get some. But so many of us are defeated before we begin, defeated by our unconscious belief systems about money. Money is a dynamic energy; it is in constant movement as the most common medium of exchange for products and services. Money is not inherently evil, as many of us have been led to believe. There is a famous misquote that we have all probably heard at one time or another in our lives, "Money is the root of all evil." The actual quote is, "For the *love* of money is the root of all evil" (1 Timothy 6:10). The latter quote makes so much more sense. Money is a neutral energy, not positive or negative. It is what we do with money or for money that determines the consequences. What we do with and for that money is a result of how we have been conditioned to think about it.

Just like our thoughts create blueprints in the creative mind that become our daily reality, we have all created a blueprint about money that we are likely unaware of. What we believe about money we experience, whether it is abundance or lack. If you believe money is the root of all evil, and you believe yourself to be a good person, subconsciously you will likely not let yourself acquire much of it, or if you do, there may be a tremendous sense of guilt mixed up in it.

Creating a new relationship with money, by reflecting on your conditioning and sorting out for yourself how you would like to earn money as well as what you would like to do with it, is an important step to creating abundance in your life.

the buck starts here . . .

Many of us don't even let ourselves think about being financially free. We associate having money with struggle and hard work, or we just don't see how we could actually get there. In order to reprogram the mind with wealth consciousness you must first identify the limiting beliefs that create your particular situation.

Begin by contemplating your current state of affairs in regard to money. Are you living hand to mouth, check to check? Are you living well but in debt, or just in debt? Are you financially secure, comfortable, or wealthy? Do you work really hard to make lots of money? Or do you work really hard and still struggle just to make ends meet?

WARRIOR WORKSHEET

"Have you ever heard someone assert that lack of money was a bit of a problem? Now hear this: A lack of money is never, ever, a problem. A lack of money is merely a symptom of what is going on underneath."

–T. HARV EKER

Describe your financial state of affairs. Be honest with yourself.

Now take a moment to think about how you feel about money. Close your eyes for a few moments and take a few deep breaths. When you are ready, begin thinking about money; not the bills you owe or what is in your bank account, just money. It can be hard to separate the thought of money from everything we associate with it. Be aware of what feelings arise in you and write them down.

Can you see now how your internal beliefs about money are creating your external reality? For the majority of us our belief systems about money were created in our childhood. The lifestyle we lived and attitudes our parents had about money conditioned our understanding of what money was, and how elusive or how abundant it was. If we heard our parents worrying about money and saw the mental, emotional, and physical struggle to make ends meet, it is likely that we are mirroring those beliefs in some way. You may now believe that there is never enough money, no matter how much you have. Or you may have decided to never be like your parents, and work your knuckles to the bone so you won't end up in a similar situation.

What about the moral issues surrounding money? That money is wicked, or that people who have money are greedy, and that the rich do terrible things with their money? Ever hear the terms "dirty money" or "filthy rich"? Have you ever been made to feel guilty or selfish about money when you wanted something, or made to feel guilty about having things at all? (Money doesn't grow on trees!) Think of it this way: can you help more people with lots of money, or with very little? Check yourself.

It is imperative to root out all of these confusing messages about money in order to be at peace with your financial situation, as well as to generate more money in your life, if that's what you're into.

living in a material world . . .

Materialism is a preoccupation with objects and comforts while neglecting other values, such as the spirit. Many of us have been warned to the point of guilt about being materialistic, that we shouldn't have too much while others go without. There is the old familiar saying, "money can't buy you happiness." This is true, of course—you can never find lasting joy outside of yourself, but it doesn't mean you must give up all your belongings to connect with your divinity, either.

All material things that we can experience in this world are the Source, or life force, manifested in multitudes of form. One of the joys of experiencing this life is taking pleasure in the things that the world has to offer us. We are the Source itself; why should the Source not take part in the bounty that is its very self? The issue is that humans, through the ego, have a tendency to identify themselves entirely with the material world. "I am not anything until I have a house or a car, or some groovy clothes." Or we use materialism to judge others. Sometimes we will go to ridiculous lengths to have money or objects, hurting ourselves and others in our haste and greed, which is obviously not a healthy relationship with money or material goods.

It is okay to want things, to have nice things, and go to fun places. It is fine to live an extravagant life, if that is what you choose. What is important is that you are in tune with your true self, your spirit self; that you experience gratitude often for the abundance you are experiencing, and that you don't have guilt or other bad feelings associated with having this wealth. It is also wonderful if you can find a way to be in service to your fellow humans, finding a way to give *of* yourself, whether or not the giving is in the form of money.

What would you do with financial abundance? What would you like to have for yourself, and what would you do for others?

digging for gold . . .

Within the mind are old, outworn ways of thinking that are likely inhibiting your financial flow. By digging out these dusty habitual thought patterns you can begin to program the mind to focus on what it is you want to experience. These inhibiting thought patterns point us to the gold within ourselves. When you can recognize what it is you, your parents, or society has conditioned you to believe, you can find compassion and forgiveness for those who have influenced you through their own unconsciousness. There are likely experiences you have had on your own that have also affected your beliefs about money. Once you can recognize your limiting beliefs, you can then begin to focus your attention, emotions, and actions on what it is you want to experience.

* * *

WARRIOR WORKSHEET

In what ways have issues with money made you feel angry?

_____

In what ways have issues with money made you feel embarrassed?

_____

In what ways have situations about money made you feel fearful?

In what ways have issues with money made you feel sad?

In what ways have issues with money made you feel guilty?

Close your eyes and ground yourself for a moment. One by one, take each experience you have had and the emotion associated with it and feel it as fully as you can. When you are ready, release it down your cord, into the Earth to be recycled. Remember to fill yourself with love and light after this release.

opulence (Inspired by Shatki Gawain's Cornucopia Meditation)

Deep down, many of us would like to experience financial abundance, but don't let ourselves think about the possibility too much because a part of us doesn't believe it will ever happen, or doesn't believe we deserve it. The following is a visualization exercise in extravagance. This exercise invites you to go into a place of boundless abundance, where there is no limit to what you can have or experience.

*   *   *

BRING YOURSELF to a calm and peaceful state of relaxation or meditation. Visualize that you are in a gorgeous field covered in colorful flowers. Soon a beautiful carriage arrives, drawn by two magnificent horses. A lovely gentleman or woman opens the door to the carriage and helps you into the lavish interior. You sit on plush cushions and are offered a delicious beverage. The carriage begins its journey, and you are entranced by the incredible scenery as you pass through the field.

Soon you arrive at a splendid mansion (or whatever else you choose, a castle or a beautiful location outdoors). You are greeted by delightful guests who are elated by your wondrous presence. It seems you are the guest of honor and are being celebrated purely because of who you are. You are led into a luxurious room, elaborately decorated with fresh flowers and extravagant furniture. There is wonderful music, and a table covered with sumptuous foods and desserts. As you sit and enjoy the feast, women and men with the faces of angels come before you and dance in your honor. You dance as well, if you feel like it. After your meal you are led to a room filled with immense amounts of riches, jewels, gold, and anything else of value you can imagine. You are told that this is yours, to do with as you please.

After spending some time in the room of riches, you walk out to a balcony. It is high on a cliff, and you can see for miles. The ocean crashes below and you are in awe of this endless greatness. You are filled with gratitude for your experience, for life itself, for all those you love, and for those magical beings who have come to celebrate you. You bow deeply to the Earth in thanks. You return the way you came, or stay for as long as you want. When you are ready, open your eyes.

Write about your experience. How did this meditation make you feel?

* * *

give it up!

Don't slip, Warriors; the power of giving is something we must not forget during our process of transformation. It is an absolutely necessary element to flow and abundance. Giving can simply mean focus and attention—give an ear to a colleague at work who's going through a divorce; give a barbecue for your closest friends. Babysit, so your friend can go out with her peeps; pick up a piece of litter. Give the trees a word of thanks for their shade on a hot day. Soul Warriors give love at every opportunity.

You can outflow loving energy to someone who needs it, to humankind, or to the world as a whole. Give your child some patience when she is driving you crazy, or be extra attentive. Cultivate the act of giving into your every day.

Giving doesn't mean you have to go to the homeless shelter and give out food, or that you have to donate money to some random charity. Of course volunteering and charitable donations are wonderful ways of giving, but if you don't have the time or money to spare, you can still give in very meaningful ways. When you pass a person on the side of the road with a sign asking for money, give him some, or give a silent blessing, outflow a little love to this stranger. Value is not just measured in dollars.

When we give selflessly, we open ourselves to the flow of unlimited abundance. We open ourselves to be given to. And, it feels good to give! There are some who would say that it is selfish to give if it makes us feel good, implying the act of giving is circumvented if one attains joy from the act of giving. Bah, humbug! What is the point of life if we are not to feel good? We should feel good as often as possible, and if helping another or giving brings one joy, then by all means, give, give, give!

When giving to others, make sure that you are also giving to yourself. Others will not benefit as much from your gift if you are not also nurturing yourself.

What are some simple ways that you already give, and other ways you can immediately begin giving?

WARRIOR METHODOLOGY

POWERFUL SOUL WARRIORS! This book is coming to an end, but your path is ever beginning. It is my hope that the ideas and exercises in this book have served your growth and understanding in some way. The following section contains more information and a few more exercises that you may choose to add to your repertoire . . .

the language of the universe

The universe, the source of all life, speaks to you all the time. It speaks in the language of symbol and synchronicity. What we usually refer to as coincidence is the secret language by which the Universal Presence, your divine self, makes contact. Take notice of these often small signals that may seem meaningless to someone else. They do not necessarily need to be deciphered, just noticed. They will let you know that you are on track, that you are plugged in, and that everything is in order. They may also warn you of what track you are on, heed these calls from your inner self. They are gifts.

first cause

We have all heard the word karma. The most common misunderstanding of the concept is that one has good or bad karma. But karma is the natural law of cause and effect, nothing more, nothing less. What comes around goes around. We are currently living karma from our thoughts and actions of the past. Our current reality is karma ever unfolding. Our present thoughts and actions are causes that are creating the next moments, days, and even years effects.

We tend to think the actions we take in the external, material world are the causes from which we reap effects. A wonderful turn-of-the-century book called *The Edinburgh Lectures* by Thomas Troward discusses what has come to be known as the "first cause." The first cause that creates an impression in the universe is in the realm of thought and feeling. The result, action experienced in our material world, is actually the effect. It is important to realize that the intention, the energy behind your thoughts and feelings, is the first cause. Any action we take is an effect of that first cause.

The energy that moves into the universe as a result of a thought or feeling will continue on its path with a similar vibration unless it gets "flipped," or changed. So, for example, if you have a negative thought (first cause), and you then get into a negative exchange with a person in your life, this is an effect of the first cause. Unless that person has the power to put an end to the negative energy pattern it is likely that they will go out into the world and have negative thought patterns and exchanges with others. This will continue until the energy pattern meets a person who will no longer perpetuate the negative energy. Likewise, if you have thoughts of joy and love, your actions (results of those thoughts) will be of a joyful, loving nature that will affect those around you, however subtly.

wheels of karma

When we do the important work of consciously creating our lives it is important to understand that there are wheels of karma still at work. There are causes, and effects of causes, and effects of effects, that you have set into motion in the past which have yet to completely play themselves out. It is easy to wonder why all the positive work you are doing doesn't have an instant effect. Or maybe you have been doing the work for a longer time and still aren't seeing the effects you want. There are karmic wheels, or energy patterns (habits) that you have put into effect in the past that may seem to counteract your current intentions. Positivity is *key* at this time. In the moments when you feel you may lose your resolve, you must concentrate your energy on love and keep your heart light. It is at these moments, when we are able to resist the old energy patterns of the past, that we are able to turn the wheels of karma and change our habits. These are the moments when we must be warriors, when we must shine the light of our will onto the new blueprint we wish to create. You must resist the urge to spiral into thought patterns that could hamper the important work you have done thus far.

back door

This next technique has many uses; it can be used for attracting something into your life, and can also be helpful for both clearing and reprogramming. The "back door" symbolizes the subconscious. This exercise gives the subconscious a distinct location (though imaginary). This imagery may be very effective and productive for some. With this exercise think clearly about what it is you desire to experience. This exercise can also be used for releasing emotional toxins or blockages, or for forgiveness. It can also be used as a self-love exercise.

Think about what it is that you would like to manifest in your life, or think of something in your life you would like to release. Focus only on one topic at a time.

Whatever it is that you would like to create, change, or build, think about it in depth and write about it here.

Be clear about your goal and identify any conflicting ideas or thoughts. Are you aware of any habits or ways of life that are in opposition to your goal? Consider this deeply for a few moments and write them here.

Take a moment to explore and write down whatever comes to mind; deep-rooted issues will likely emerge as the light of attention is directed towards them. Once you discover these hidden beliefs you can be more aware of what new programming you want to create in their place.

back-door meditation

 BRING YOURSELF to a calm and centered place of awareness using the previous warrior methods or your own. Observe the breath for a few minutes.

FOR RELEASE: Bring to the forefront of your mind your intention to release subconscious thought patterns, habits, and emotions—old unsupportive beliefs that you want to remove from your identity that may be impeding your ability to attract the desired circumstances. Imagine that there is a small door in the back of your head/mind; this is the door to your subconscious. Open the door and imagine removing what you want to release. Feel the emotion that may be attached to the memory. Honor these energies, offer them peace and release. For example, "Peace. Thank you for bringing attention to a part of me that just wants to be loved." Send these old energy patterns down your grounding cord into the Earth to be recycled. After you are done, close the door.

Deep patterns have a harder time changing. Don't give up if they don't release the first time. You may have to repeat this process several times to release old belief patterns. Some say the potential for the unwanted pattern never really leaves your subconscious space. It just loses power to the positive habit/belief that it is being replaced by. Either way, taking action is what's important: recognizing whatever may be holding you back, consciously taking power from it, and giving that power to something else.

Important: When you are doing the release part of this exercise it is very important to substitute positive energy for the negative or the space may be filled with the same energy that was removed.

FOR ATTRACTING/MANIFESTING: Imagine what it is you desire to bring into your life. Really feel the essence of what it is you want to bring or change in your life. Engage the senses. Use an intention or affirmation. When you feel that you have created the picture you would like to see, say to yourself, "I manifest this or something better" and open the back door. Imagine putting the whole of what you have just visualized into this subconscious space. You may then direct the subconscious to "please attend to this." And smile.

* * *

Trust that what you have sent out into the realm of the subconscious will be taken care of, that you will be guided by the universe and by your own intuition towards that which is ideal for your experience and growth.

manifest maps

Creating a powerful life is an ongoing process. We are constantly creating our lives whether we are aware of it or not. It is important that we habituate consciously creating. If you don't find joy in the focused act of conscious creation, you are likely out of alignment with it. Make it fun!

One easy and relatively inexpensive thing that you can do immediately is to start buying magazines on the subject of anything you are really interested in manifesting and experiencing in your life. Get subscriptions to the magazines you truly enjoy. One way to activate your creative powers is to focus your attention on the things you want to manifest, by regularly looking at images that represent your visions, and by learning whatever you can about the subject.

Create a manifest map. Cut out pictures of things that symbolize the life you are creating for yourself. Get a glue stick and a piece of posterboard or corkboard and place images and words on it. Put it up in your house somewhere where you can see it daily. Add to it often, keep it fresh. This process can help bring abstract thoughts into a more tangible sensory experience. The thought-form becomes denser, with visual focus, giving the mind the extra energy it needs to make something become more realistic.

BLESSINGS ON YOUR JOURNEY!

affirmation and resource guide

REMEMBER TO ALWAYS use the present tense when creating your affirmations. The future is always in the future, and what you experience is always in the present.

Always word your affirmations in the positive. Invoking positive feelings when using affirmations strengthens them.

Writing them down helps you remember the exact wording. Writing and/or saying them repeatedly helps by creating the repetition needed for reprogramming.

Use the following affirmations as they are, or use them as examples to create just the right affirmation for you.

health

* I have abundant energy, vitality, and well-being.
* I am healthy in all aspects of my being.
* I am grateful for my beautiful temple.
* I am always able to maintain my ideal weight.
* I am filled with energy to do all the daily activities in my life.

* My mind is at peace.
* I am in alignment with health, wealth, and wisdom.
* I love and care for my body and it cares for me.
* I am already whole.
* Every cell in my body vibrates with energy and health.
* I am healthy, healed, and whole.
* I choose health.
* I naturally make choices that are good for me.
* I take loving care of my body and my body responds with health and an abundance of energy.

abundance

* I am a success in all that I do.
* Everything I touch returns riches to me.
* I am always productive.
* I respect my abilities and always work to my full potential.
* I am constantly adding to my income.
* I always spend money wisely.
* I always have enough money for all that I need.
* I am rewarded for all the work I do.
* My income is constantly increasing.
* Abundance flows effortlessly to me.
* I am a money magnet, and prosperity and opportunity are drawn to me.
* I know that life is abundant and I accept abundance in my life now.
* I have access to infinite resources.

relationships

* All my relationships are now loving and harmonious.
* I now attract the perfect partner into my life.
* I deserve love and happiness.
* I attract only loving and uplifting people into my life.

* My friends are mutually loving and supportive.
* My relationship with _____ gets stronger and more loving every day.
* I love and accept myself the way I am and I love and accept others as they are.
* I make friends easily wherever I go.
* I easily forgive all those who need forgiving and I forgive myself.
* Forgiving makes me feel light and free.
* As I learn to love myself I find it easier to forgive.

love and awareness
* I am at peace with the universe.
* I love and accept myself.
* I am always safe.
* I always feel protected.
* I acknowledge all of my feelings because I am in touch with my feelings.
* I honor my feelings and emotions.
* I am surrounded with loving, caring people in my life.
* I am at peace with myself.
* I am always in harmony with the universe.
* I am filled with the love of the universal divine truth.
* I am at peace with all those around me.
* I am at one with the inner child in me.
* I am free to be myself.
* I am a loving person.
* I am responsible for my own spiritual growth.
* I now choose thoughts that nourish and support me in a loving and positive way.
* I have given myself permission to be at one with the universe.
* I am worthy of love.
* I am surrounded by love.
* I love and accept myself exactly as I am.

* I know that I deserve love and I accept it now.
* I am a loving, beautiful, creative person, which is reflected in my relationships with others.
* Loving myself unconditionally brings healing and an abundance of love into my life.
* Love flows through my body and radiates out from me in all directions.
* I go with the flow and my life is filled with joy.
* I am grateful for all the wonderful things I already have in my life and those that are yet to come.
* The more I love, the more that love is returned to me.
* I nurture my inner child.
* I am responsible for my life and always maintain the power I need to be positive and joyful.
* I trust my divine self to lead me in the right path.
* My being is my sustenance.
* I am always connected with the divine love of the universe.

Read These!!!
Powerful and Profound Books

The Seven Spiritual Laws of Success by Deepak Chopra

Creative Visualization by Shakti Gawain

Secrets of the Millionaire Mind by T. Harv Eker

The Edinburgh Lectures on Mental Science by Thomas Troward

God I Am by Peter O. Erbe

Metaphysics: The Science of Life by Anthony Fisichella

The Alchemist by Paulo Coelho

Enchanted Love by Marianne Williamson

The Power of Now by Eckhart Tolle

The Tao of Sexology by Steven Chang

Succulent Wild Woman by SARK

The Dark Side of the Light Chasers by Debbie Ford

The Book of Mirdad by Mikhail Naimy

acknowledgments

I would like to give a word of thanks to my punk-rock publisher Soft Skull and Mr. Richard Nash for this amazing opportunity. Thanks also to my editor Anne Connolly for helping me make it just right. I have deep gratitude for Michael Fusco, Neuwirth design, and for all the Soft Skull/Counterpoint staff who worked on this project. Mucho love to Celia Herrera at urbanbricks.com for the original cover design idea, and for my fly ass website, www.urbansoulwarrior.com. To my mother Theresa Carrillo, thank you for your undying faith in me, even when my ideas seemed real crazy. To my beautiful grandmother Ortencia Carrillo; it is through you that we are here. To my sister Carolina Jaramillo, you are an amazing mother and friend. To my father Dr. Gregory Jaramillo, thank you for your support throughout my life. And to my golden child Kaliya, yes, you are the center of my universe. To my home girls, know this, I couldn't have done this without you! Jlove, for all you have done, since day one. Vania Gallegos, my sista from anotha motha. Asia, light and lovely strength. Faatma, veggies rock! Christina, generous heart. Celia, da realest. Victoria, my intergalactic soul sibling. Marcelina, for the good ol' days. Peace to the Gypsies! Much respect to Fire Lily and Basheba. Love to my Brooklyn crew, Samara, Gia, and Dalila. Big love to Kinh for always serving up light on a platter, and for being an amazing mirror. Rest, grandfather, see you in the skies. Peace to Earth Mama, thank you for loving us even when we act like some badass kids. Love to the trees, and the air, and the sun and water. I & I love LIFE! Peace.